# NORFOLK & WESTERN STEAM
(The Last 25 Years)

By Ron Rosenberg
with Eric H. Archer
© 1973 by Ron Rosenberg
Published by
Quadrant Press, Incorporated
Room 707N 19 West 44th Street
New York, New York 10036

3rd Printing
ISBN 0-915276-00-3

# Acknowledgments

Our fine cover painting is the work of Howard Fogg, noted railroad illustrator. Howard's brush captured a dramatic episode in the glory days of steam on the N&W — the J-powered *Powhatan Arrow* overtaking a laboring A-class 2-6-6-4 on a wintry day in the Blue Ridge mountains of Virginia. A high-quality 16"x22" lithograph of this scene is available for $5.50 from MILEPOST PUBLISHING CO., INC. P.O. BOX 5315 Grand Central Station, New York, New York, 10017. MILEPOST also offers prints of Fogg paintings of the Chief, the Crescent Limited, the Ambassador, and the Twentieth Century Limited behind conventional steam locomotives.

For esthetic reasons, we omitted the credit line on our title page. We are indebted to Don Ball, Jr., author of PORTRAIT OF THE RAILS for the use of that photo and many others in this book.

Our thanks are also extended to the N&W's Public Relations Department, to John H. White, Jr. of the Smithsonian Institution, to Bob Paltos of Simmons-Boardman, and to Freeman Hubbard of *Railroad Magazine* for the use of material in which they have a proprietary interest.

We are likewise grateful to John Briggs and Karl R. Zimmermann for the contribution which their photos made to our chronicle of steam on the N&W.

Marvin H. Cohen, one of our photo contributors, deserves our thanks for several reasons. Marv is also our tireless proofreader, and liaison with our printer.

During the preparation of this book, we often called upon our friend Arnold B. Joseph to supply us with backdate copies of railroad magazines. Should you have similar needs, we suggest you write to Arnold at Apt. D-17, 2512 Tratman Ave., Bronx, N. Y. 10461.

We also owe thanks to our friends Thomas H. Dressler, Jeffrey K. Winslow, Howard Pincus and Mike Pearsall for labors expended during the production of this work.

The majority of photos used in this book were made available to us by the following friends who would welcome enquiries from others interested in photo purchases:

C. W. Jernstrom, 822 Pelham Drive, Ft. Wayne, IN 46825
Allan Sherry, 5410 Netherland Avenue, Riverdale, NY 10471
Harold K. Vollrath, 8938 Maple Dr., Shawnee-Mission, KS 66207
Charles E. Winters, 3717 NE 49th St., Kansas City, MO 64119

Finally, we owe our wives Ellie and Joann a large thank-you for months of forebearance.

|  |  |
|---|---|
| R.B.R. | New York City |
| E.H.A. | December 11, 1972 |

# Introduction

Since its formation, the Norfolk and Western Railway has remained singularly dedicated to one economic mission: the transport of bituminous coal from collieries in mountainous West Virginia to markets miles distant beyond the Ohio River, or along the Atlantic littoral. The volume of this traffic and the many geographic obstacles to be surmounted in its profitable movement forced the N&W to become acutely aware of the necessity for powerful steam locomotives at a very early date. Increasing business, particularly the upsurge concurrent with World War One focused the N&W's attention on new design criteria, namely, serviceability and ease of maintenance. The hard times of the thirties made these two virtues actual necessities in the eyes of the railway's management, and even more inventive genius was applied to the refinement of the reciprocating steam locomotive.

The results of this effort are well known to any rail enthusiast. In the five-year span between 1936 and 1941, the N&W's own Roanoke Shops turned out the most powerful dual-service articulateds with six driving axles, the ultimate refinement of the 2-8-8-2 mallet compound, *and* the most powerful 4-8-4's ever built. Furthermore, the railway's management refused to curtail experimentation and improvement simply because steam traction was no longer fashionable, and the N&W pioneered in the development of coal-fired steam power as late as 1954!

The Norfolk and Western's unusual dedication and continued faith gave railfans one final chance to see big steam at work on a major trunk-line railroad, as late as 1960. If you witnessed steam's final drama, we hope you find this book a fitting remembrance of the last act on the Blue Ridge.

# Contents

|  |  |  | *Page* |
|---|---|---|---|
| Part One: Older Power | | | 1 |
| G1 | 2-8-0 | | 3 |
| W2 | 2-8-0 | | 5 |
| W6 | 0-8-0T | | 7 |
| V1 | 4-6-0 | | 9 |
| M | 4-8-0 | | 11 |
| M1 | 4-8-0 | | 14 |
| M2 | 4-8-0 | | 15 |
| E,E1 | 4-6-2 | | 17 |
| E2 | 4-6-2 | | 18 |
| E3 | 4-6-2 | (ex-PRR) | 20 |
| K1 | 4-8-2 | | 21 |
| K2 | 4-8-2 | (U.S.R.A.) | 23 |
| K3 | 4-8-2 | | 28 |
| Z1 | 2-6-6-2 | | 29 |
| Y2 | 2-8-8-2 | | 32 |
| Y3 | 2-8-8-2 | (U.S.R.A.) | 34 |
| Y4 | 2-8-8-2 | | 36 |
| Y5 | 2-8-8-2 | | 38 |
| Part Two: Modern Power | | | 41 |
| A | 2-6-6-4 | | 45 |
| Y6 | 2-8-8-2 | | 53 |
| Y6a | 2-8-8-2 | | 54 |
| Y6b | 2-8-8-2 | | 55 |
| J | 4-8-4 | | 68 |
| J1 | 4-8-4 | | 73 |
| M2 | 4-8-0 | Automatic | 77 |
| S1 | 0-8-0 | (ex-C&O) | 79 |
| S1a | 0-8-0 | (N&W copy) | 82 |
| TE1 | C-C+C-C | Turbine | 85 |
| Part Three: Wandering Giants | | | 88 |
| Part Four: Smaller Surplus | | | 91 |
| Part Five: Models Made | | | 93 |

# Part 1: Older Power

Heretofore, most photographic treatises on Norfolk & Western steam power have concentrated on the renowned A, J and Y6 locos constructed by the road's own Roanoke Shops since 1936. These newer locos were what attracted most railfan photographers to trackside, and they were clearly more conspicuous, more glamorous, and better publicized than the balance of the railway's motive power roster. Few shutterbugs took notice of the older locos until after World War Two, when their numbers were waning rapidly.

Knowing rail enthusiasts listened to the N&W's expressions of confidence in the future of steam locomotion, but gave greater credence to developments elsewhere. Baldwin and Alco eschewed steam loco production altogether, and Lima, the surviving U.S. trade supplier outshopped 36 steamers in 1948, 31 in 1949, and none thereafter. Everywhere, steam fans subconsciously realized the end was near, and *any* steam loco, however unkempt and homely, was now a worthwhile photographic subject.

What remains today? Five N&W locos built before 1935 have been preserved for public display. G1 2-8-0 number 6 is in the Transportation Museum at Roanoke, Va., G1 7 is at the Municipal Fair Grounds at Bluefield, W. Va., and sister 22 is preserved at the Olin-Mathieson plant in Saltville, Va. One of the many 4-8-0's may still be seen: 433 at Abingdon, Va. Finally, E2a 578 at the Ohio Railway Museum in Worthington, Ohio is the only N&W steam loco still operable at this writing.

Fortunately, some talented photographers recognized the peril in time, and the next 38 pages are our subjective attempt to redress the scanty coverage previously accorded to older Norfolk and Western steam motive power. OPPOSITE: Streamlined K2a 136 under the N&W catenary at Bluefield, West Virginia in June, 1947. At this time, Norfolk & Western freights from this point west to Ieager, West Virginia were worked by jackshaft electrics.

*(Throughout this work, photos not otherwise credited are from the Ron Rosenberg collection).*

## ROSTER RECAPITULATION: OLDER LOCOMOTIVES

| CLASS | TYPE | 1936 | 1942 | 1944 | 1949 | 1953 | 1954 | 1956 | 1961 | All-time Total |
|---|---|---|---|---|---|---|---|---|---|---|
| E | 4-6-2 | 4 | 0 | 0 | 0 | 0 | 0 | 0 | 0 | 5 |
| E1 | 4-6-2 | 14 | 0 | 0 | 0 | 0 | 0 | 0 | 0 | 15 |
| E2 | 4-6-2 | 37 | 27 | 27 | 25 | 4 | 3 | 2 | 0 | 37 |
| E3 | 4-6-2 | 5 | 5 | 5 | 0 | 0 | 0 | 0 | 0 | 5 |
| G1 | 2-8-0 | 9 | 6 | 6 | 2 | 2 | 2 | 0 | 0 | ? |
| K1 | 4-8-2 | 16 | 16 | 16 | 16 | 16 | 16 | 16 | 0 | 16 |
| K2 | 4-8-2 | 22 | 22 | 22 | 22 | 22 | 22 | 22 | 0 | 22 |
| K3 | 4-8-2 | 10 | 10 | 10 | 0 | 0 | 0 | 0 | 0 | 10 |
| M | 4-8-0 | 55 | 41 | 40 | 36 | 22 | 16 | 15 | 1 | 125 |
| M1 | 4-8-0 | 28 | 17 | 17 | 0 | 0 | 0 | 0 | 0 | 100 |
| M2 | 4-8-0 | 61 | 60 | 60 | 60 | 34 | 20 | 16 | 0 | 61 |
| V1 | 4-6-0 | 5 | 4 | 4 | 2 | 0 | 0 | 0 | 0 | 17 |
| W2 | 2-8-0 | 56 | 45 | 44 | 35 | 5 | 0 | 0 | 0 | 127 |
| W6 | 0-8-0T | 9 | 6 | 6 | 6 | 6 | 4 | 4 | 0 | 12 |
| Y2 | 2-8-8-2 | 31 | 31 | 31 | 10 | 0 | 0 | 0 | 0 | 31 |
| Y3 | 2-8-8-2 | 50 | 50 | 50 | 31 | 31 | 31 | 31 | 0 | 50 |
| Y3a | 2-8-8-2 | 30 | 30 | 30 | 30 | 30 | 30 | 30 | 0 | 30 |
| Y4 | 2-8-8-2 | 10 | 10 | 10 | 10 | 10 | 10 | 10 | 0 | 10 |
| Y5 | 2-8-8-2 | 20 | 19 | 19 | 19 | 19 | 19 | 19 | 8 | 20 |
| Z1 | 2-6-6-2 | 153 | 116 | 116 | 105 | 82 | 60 | 53 | 0 | 190 |
| | | 625 | 515 | 513 | 409 | 306 | 233 | 218 | 9 | |

# 2-8-0 G1

These diminutive Consolidations were supplanted in mainline service shortly after delivery by W2 2-8-0's and M-class 4-8-0's. Nonetheless, the G1's extremely light axle loadings assured the class of a place on the N&W's roster until the advent of diesel switchers. Locos 6 and 7 served into the 'fifties on seasonal cattle extras between Bluefield and Honaker, Virginia over a line marked by several spindly timber trestles. RIGHT: 7 at Bluefield, W. Va., June 1947.

**THE 1936 ROSTER:**

4-7, 301, 302 (Baldwin, 1897)

| Driv. Diam. | Total Loco Weight | Weight On Drivers | Cylinders Bore x Stroke | Boiler Pressure | Tractive Effort |
|---|---|---|---|---|---|
| 50" | 120,785 lbs. | 107,000 lbs. | 20"x24" | 180 psi | 29,376 lbs. |

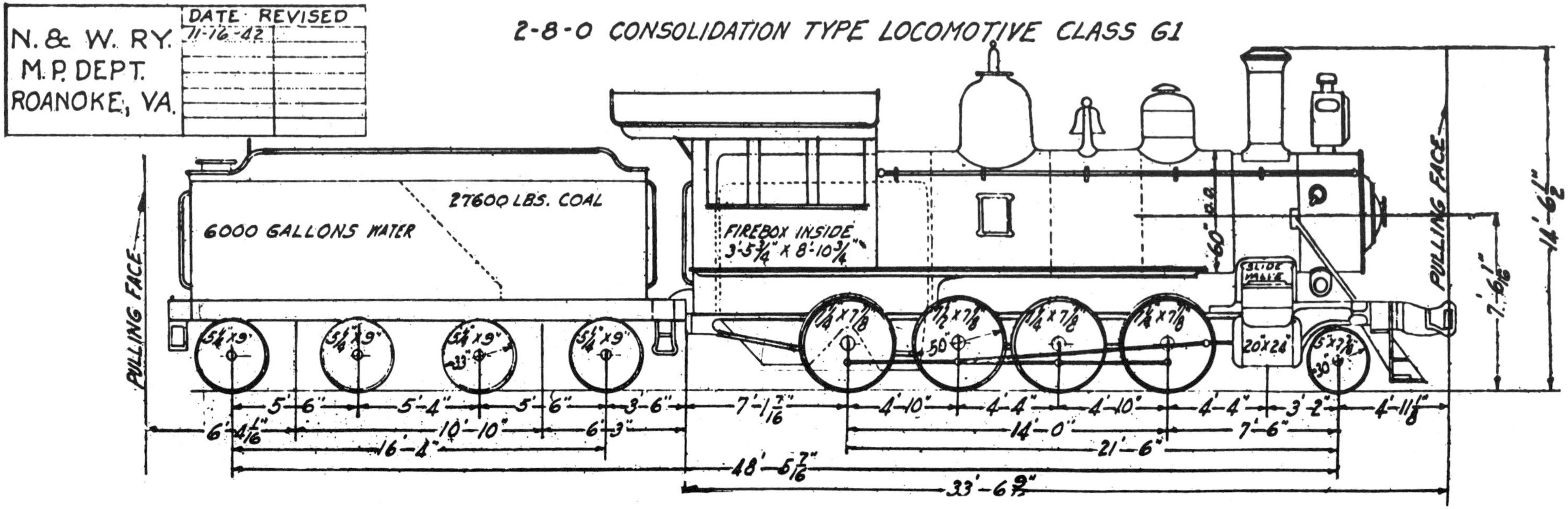

The G-'s boiler and mechanism were overwhelmed by an old-style N&W headlight, shotgun stack, steam dome, and capacious cab more suited for a high-wheeled 4-4-2. *Collection of Harold K. Vollrath.*

# 2-8-0 W2

The healthiest 2-8-0's on the N&W would have been considered only light Consolidations on many other railroads, but the W2's were about one-third more powerful than the G1's. The longevity of this class was enhanced by the interchangeability of many parts between those locos and the slightly newer class M 4-8-0's.

THE 1936 ROSTER:

673, 674, 678-680 (Baldwin, 1905), 684, 686, 690, 692, 693, 695, 697, 698, 701, 702, 704 (Richmond, 1905), 716, 719 (Richmond, 1904), 722, 728 (Baldwin, 1904), 731 (Roanoke Shops, 1904), 735, 746, 750, 752, 756, 758, 759 (Baldwin, 1903), 766, 769, (Cooke, 1903), 778, 779, 788-790 (Richmond, 1903), 794 (Baldwin, 1903), 867 (Roanoke Shops, 1903), 882 (Richmond, 1901), 884-887, 892 (Richmond, 1902), 910, 914 (Baldwin, 1902), 915, 917 (Baldwin, 2903), 922 (Richmond, 1902), 930, 940, 943, 944, 946 (Cooke, 1903)

| Driv. Diam. | Total Loco Weight | Weight On Drivers | Cylinders Bore x Stroke | Boiler Pressure | Tractive Effort |
|---|---|---|---|---|---|
| 56" | 175,100 lbs | 157,850 lbs. | 21"x30" | 200 psi | 40,163 |

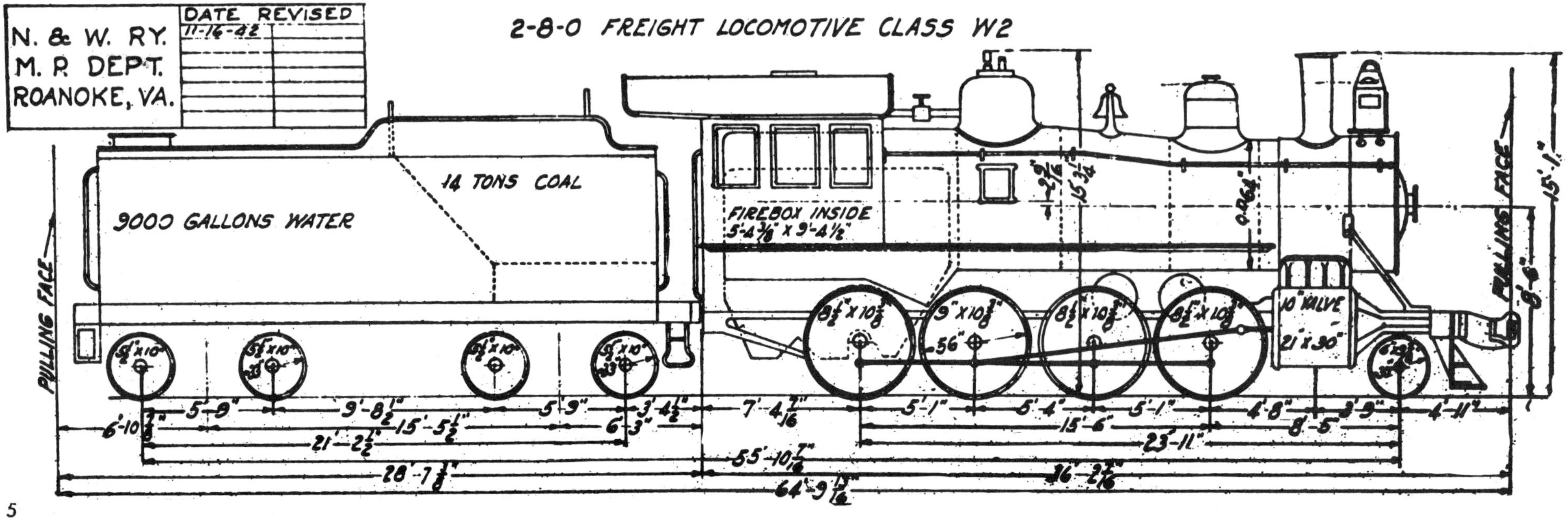

This shot of W2 690 illustrates an amusing contrast in appliances. Note the modern Pyle-National headlight perched on a bracket suitable for a beer keg, and the two old-fashioned one-lung air pumps.

W2 885 and crew posed for a portrait at Columbus, Ohio in August, 1954. The locomotive was obviously engaged in switching duties, usual for this class in the last years of steam on the N&W. The ancient headlight has been retained, but the short stack and cinder screen are recent "improvements". *Both photos, collection of Harold K. Vollrath.*

# 0-8-0T
# W6

Shop switchers were used to move dead locomotives and detached tenders between repair and service facilities. These shifters were kept as short as possible to enable them to fit onto a turntable or transfer table with an entire loco and tender in tow. The N&W's shop switchers carried a couple of hours' supply of water in a saddle tank, and two tons of coal in a bunker behind the cab. Most such locos were rebuilt from road power, and the W6's were no exception. *Collection of Harold K. Vollrath.*

THE 1936 ROSTER:
800, 802, 804, 809 (Baldwin, 1898 as W 2-8-0)
821, 825, 830 (Baldwin, 1900 as W1 2-8-0)
839 (Roanoke Shops, 1900 as W1 2-8-0)
860 (Richmond, 1901 as W1 2-8-0)

| Driv. Diam. | Total Loco Weight | Weight On Drivers | Cylinders Bore x Stroke | Boiler Pressure | Tractive Effort |
|---|---|---|---|---|---|
| 56" | 186,900 lbs. | 186,900 lbs. | 21"x30" | 200 psi | 40,163 lbs. |

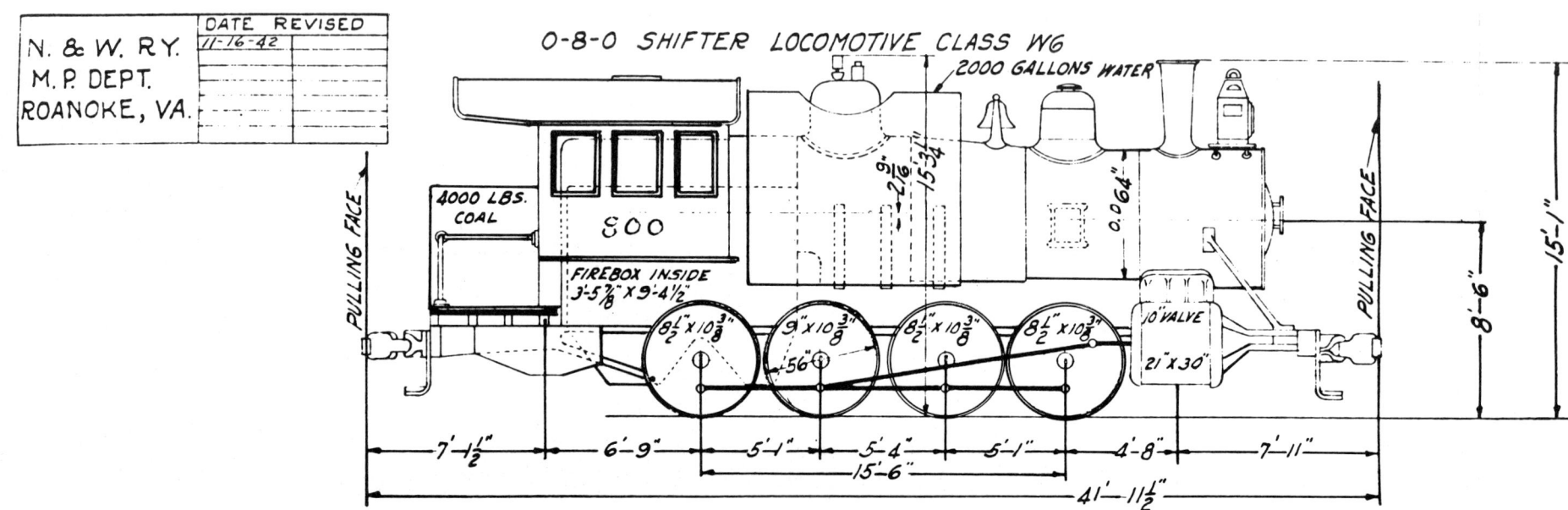

Shifter 821 occupied scarcely a third of the turntable at Roanoke's Shaffers Crossing engine house. That rectangular aperture in the cab side no doubt eased maintenance of the injector, but must have admitted quite a draft in the wintertime. Note the gooseneck lamp tucked under the eaves of the cab to illuminate the rear platform. This loco was later renumbered to 12 to clear a series of numbers for some GP-9's delivered in 1958. *John Briggs Photo.*

# 4-6-0
# V1

Ten-wheelers were popular dual-service locos on many American railroads, but not on the N&W, simply because their slipperiness and low tractive effort made them unsuitable for mineral train service. Surprisingly, five N&W 4-6-0's survived the depression, and four soldiered on through World War Two. RIGHT: 954 stored at Norfolk in 1948. *Collection of Harold K. Vollrath.*

THE 1936 ROSTER:

950, 951, 954, 956, 960 (Baldwin, 1900)

| Driv. Diam. | Total Loco Weight | Weight On Drivers | Cylinders Bore x Stroke | Boiler Pressure | Tractive Effort |
|---|---|---|---|---|---|
| 62" | 162,350 lbs. | 128,025 lbs. | 19½"x28" | 200 psi | 29,193 lbs. |

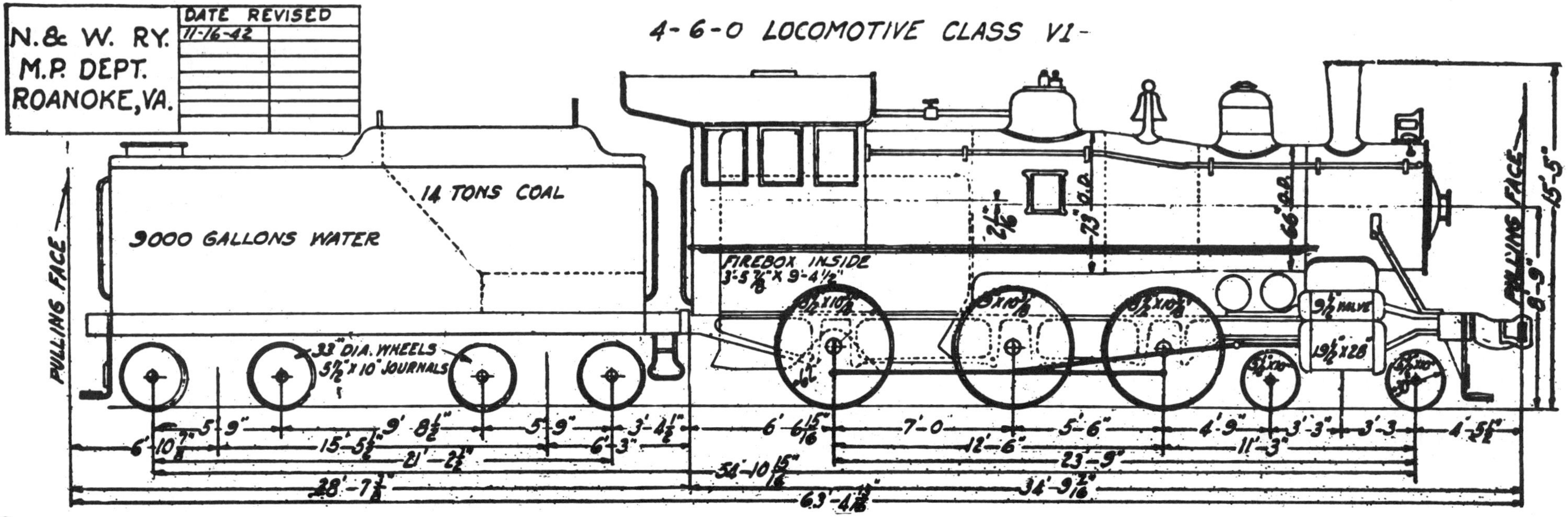

This superb photo from the Harold K. Vollrath collection shows the opposite side of the same locomotive under steam some twelve years earlier. The standard N&W lettering scheme of the 'thirties called for the small road name spelled out on the cab side, and no markings on the flanks of the tender.

# 4-8-0 M

N&W fans found 4-8-0's unremarkable, since the road possessed about two-thirds of the twelve-wheelers in America. However, there is ample photographic evidence of the attraction which the M-class held for visiting rail enthusiasts unjaded by familiarity with the wheel arrangement. The ubiquitous M's made up coal drags, whipped way freights over the main, wandered down sylvan branch lines on the point of mixed trains, and shunted sleepers and head-end cars while unknowing passengers slept. RIGHT: 464 tacks on a diner at Roanoke in 1941.

THE 1936 ROSTER:
375, 376, 379, 382-384. 388, 392-394, 404, 405, 407, 410, 411, 413, 419, 421, 422, 423 (Richmond, 1906), 427, 429, 431, 433, 434, 439, 442, 444, 445, 447-449 (Richmond, 1907), 451-457, 459, 462-464, 467-469, 471, 475, 477, 482, 484, 488, 490, 495, 496 (Baldwin, 1906)

| Driv. Diam. | Total Loco Weight | Weight On Drivers | Cylinders Bore x Stroke | Boiler Pressure | Tractive Effort |
|---|---|---|---|---|---|
| 56" | 200,000 lbs. | 168,000 lbs. | 21"x30" | 200 psi | 40,163 lbs. |

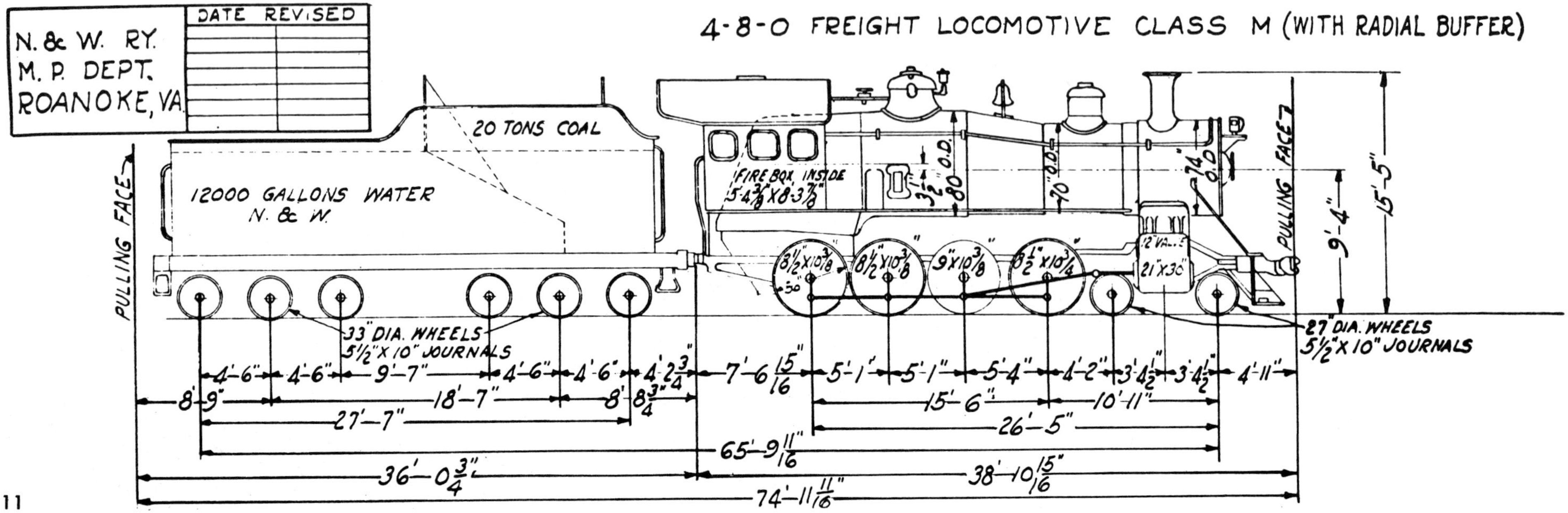

## M'S ON MIXED TRAINS

Many photographic pilgrimages in the 'fifties focused on class M 4-8-0's in mixed service, particularly on trains 201 and 202 on their 110-mile turn between Abingdon and West Jefferson, and the more accessible nine-mile run linking Christiansburg on the main line with Blacksburg, home of the Virginia Polytechnic Institute. At right, 382 eases up to the water plug at Abingdon. *Marvin H. Cohen photo.* Below, 475 hustles freight and passengers past the Christiansburg depot. *Collection of Harold K. Vollrath.*

Most steam photographers were portraitists, but an exceptional few sought the right circumstances to capture the appearance of the iron horse at work. Don Ball, Jr. shot the 422 making up a freight during one of his many photo safaris into Norfolk and Western territory.

# 4-8-0 M1

**THE 1936 ROSTER:**
1002, 1005, 1006, 1012, 1017, 1021, 1025, 1026, 1034, 1040, 1045, 1048 (Baldwin, 1907), 1050, 1051, 1055, 1057, 1059, 1060, 1062, 1063, 1070, 1077, 1081, 1083, 1090-1092, 1098 (Richmond, 1907)

Specifications same as class M.

On paper, the M1's were virtually identical to the M's, but the subclass was not as well regarded by the Norfolk and Western. We speculate that the M1's Walschaert valve gear was a cause of the dissatisfaction, but we really aren't sure. Several Southern short lines were nonetheless happy to acquire M1's second-hand. Above, 1012 on the ready track at Columbus in 1936.
*Collection of Harold K. Vollrath.*

# 4-8-0 M2

4-8-0's were dubbed Mastodons on some railroads, and the M2's of the N&W most certainly deserved that appellation. These brutes were by far the heaviest twelve-wheelers ever constructed, outweighing the nearest competition by almost 25 tons. The M2's were such fine steamers and so sure-footed that the N&W extensively altered two of the class right after the war in a realistic attempt to make the class economically competitive with diesel switchers. What other forty-year old steamers warranted such an investment? *Right, from C. W. Jernstrom.*

THE 1936 ROSTER:
M2 class
1100-1149 (Baldwin, 1910)
M2a class
1150-1160 (Roanoke Shops, 1911)

| Driv. Diam. | Total Loco Weight | Weight On Drivers | Cylinders Bore x Stroke | Boiler Pressure | Tractive Effort |
|---|---|---|---|---|---|
| 56" | 262,000 lbs. | 222,000 lbs. | 24"x30" | 200 psi | 52,457 lbs. |

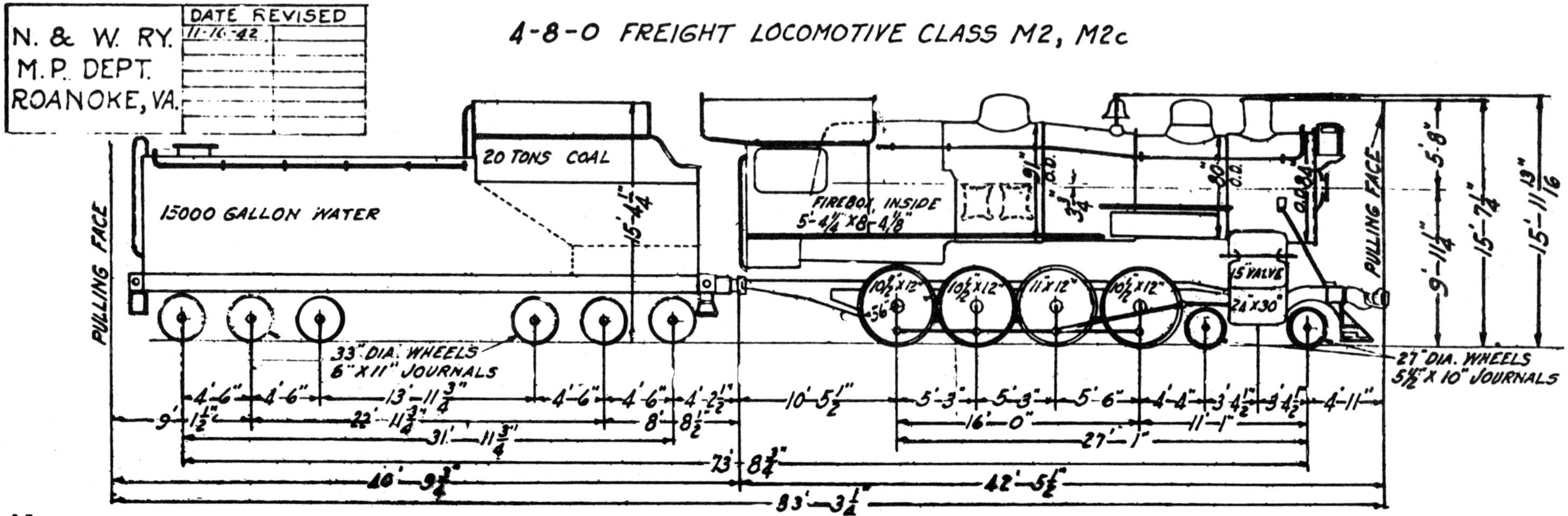

15

The broadside of the 1155 at right proves the diagram is right. That tender is almost as long as the locomotive! *Photo from C. W. Jernstrom.* Below, the 1129 hustles empty hoppers westbound through Vinton, Va. Worthington type BL feedwater heaters were rarely installed on smaller non-articulated N&W locos.

# 4-6-2 E, E1

The N&W's two oldest classes of Pacifics succumbed to economics and increasing auto travel in the '30's. Like the Norfolk and Western's delicate 4-4-2's, every E and E1 went to the torch. At right, 596 is shown in service at Bristol, Virginia in 1925. Below, the same loco shortly before dismantling at Roanoke some fourteen years later. *Both, Collection of Harold K. Vollrath.*

THE 1936 ROSTER:
E class
595, 597-599 (Richmond, 1905)
E1 class
580, 583, 584, 592, 593 (Baldwin, 1907)

| Driv. Diam. | Total Loco Weight | Weight On Drivers | Cylinders Bore x Stroke | Boiler Pressure | Tractive Effort |
|---|---|---|---|---|---|
| 68" | 196,253 lbs. | unknown | 20"x28" | 200 psi | 28,000 lbs. |
| 68" | 247,000 lbs. | 166,000 lbs. | 20"x28" | 200 psi | 34,425 lbs. |

# 4-6-2
# E2

Over half of N&W's 4-6-2's were in class E2, and suffixes a and b simply differentiated later Baldwin and Roanoke products from the original locos built by Richmond Locomotive Works. The upsurge of traffic incident to World War Two stayed the departure of the E2's from N&W rails temporarily, but only a few of the passenger runs remaining after the conflict were within the capacity of a Pacific locomotive.

THE 1936 ROSTER:
E2 class
574-579 (Richmond, 1910)
E2a class
553-573 (Baldwin, 1912)

E2b class
543-547 (Roanoke Shops, 1914)
548-552 (Roanoke Shops, 1913)

| Driv. Diam. | Total Loco Weight | Weight On Drivers | Cylinders Bore x Stroke | Boiler Pressure | Tractive Effort |
|---|---|---|---|---|---|
| 70" | 247,000 lbs. | 166,000 lbs. | 22½"x28" | 200 psi | 34,425 lbs. |

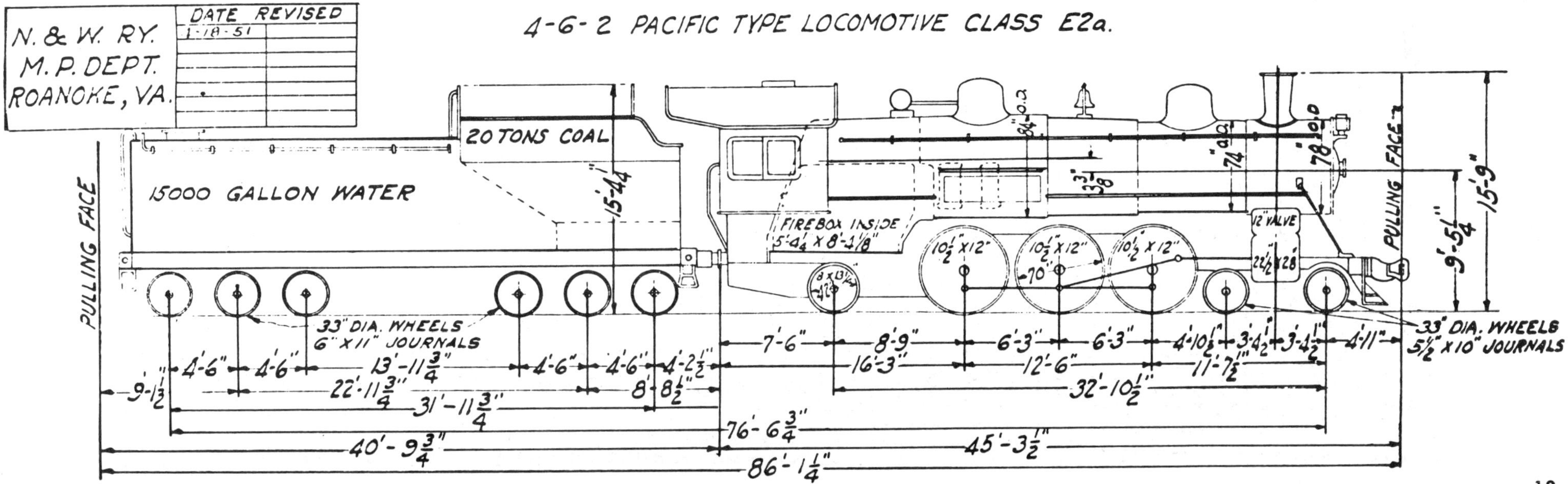

RIGHT: This view of 566 illustrates a notable peculiarity of the E2's — none ever received a modern cross-compound air pump.

BELOW: E2a 557 leads a classic two-car local train through the verdant Virginia countryside back in 1951. Why spend $180,000 for a GP-7 to perform the same task? *Both photos, collection of Harold K. Vollrath.*

# 4-6-2 E3

The handful of Pacifics in class E3 weren't a Roanoke design at all, but were purchased surplus from the Pennsylvania Railroad in the early '30s.

LEFT: This photo reveals a few alterations made by the new owner. The much larger tender is readily apparent. The new pilot, headlight, number plate, spoked pilot wheels and low-water alarm are much more difficult to spot.

| THE 1936 ROSTER: | Driv. | Total Loco | Weight On | Cylinders | Boiler | Tractive |
|---|---|---|---|---|---|---|
| 500-504 (Baldwin, 1913 as PRR class K-3) | Diam. | Weight | Drivers | Bore x Stroke | Pressure | Effort |
| (Ex-PRR 8657, 7075, 7090, 7308, 8658) | 80" | 293,600 lbs. | 196,300 lbs. | 26"x26" | 205 psi | 38,283 lbs. |

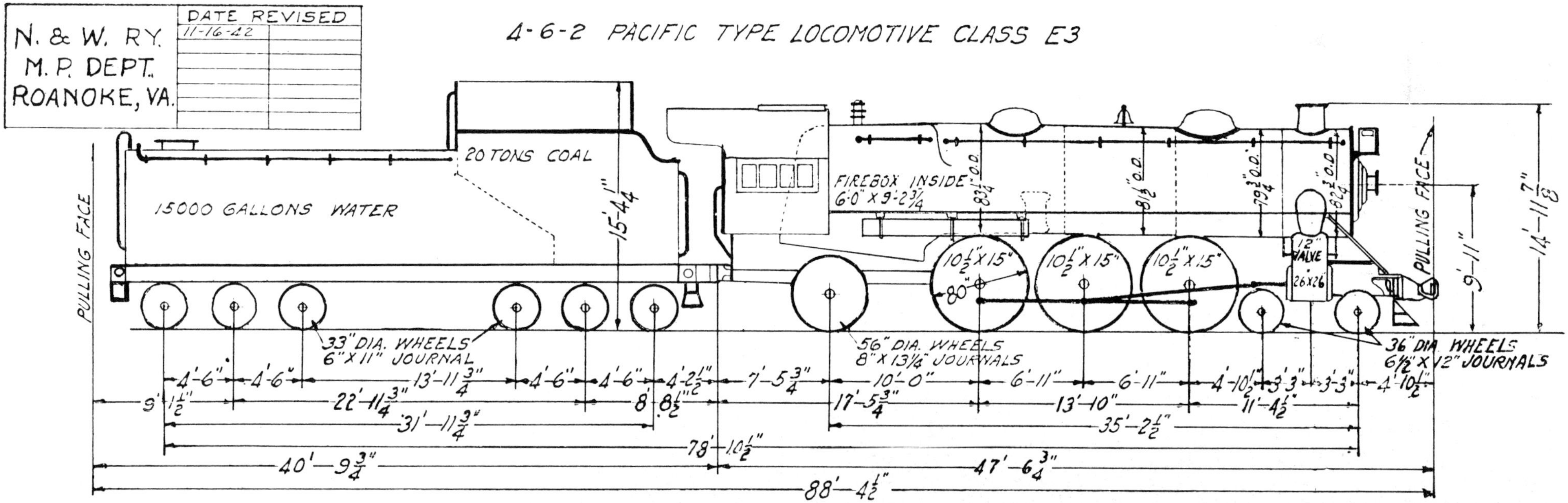

# 4-8-2 K1

The N&W's first Mountain types were the oldest class of steamers which remained intact right up 'till the receipt of large numbers of diesel road switchers in the late 'fifties. What saved the K1's was an extensive modernization right after the war. The massive sand dome and the "sports model" cab shown in the photos were the most obvious results of the shopping, but the changes were more than skin-deep. Much more important were improvements to the lubrication system. *Right, from the Vollrath collection.*

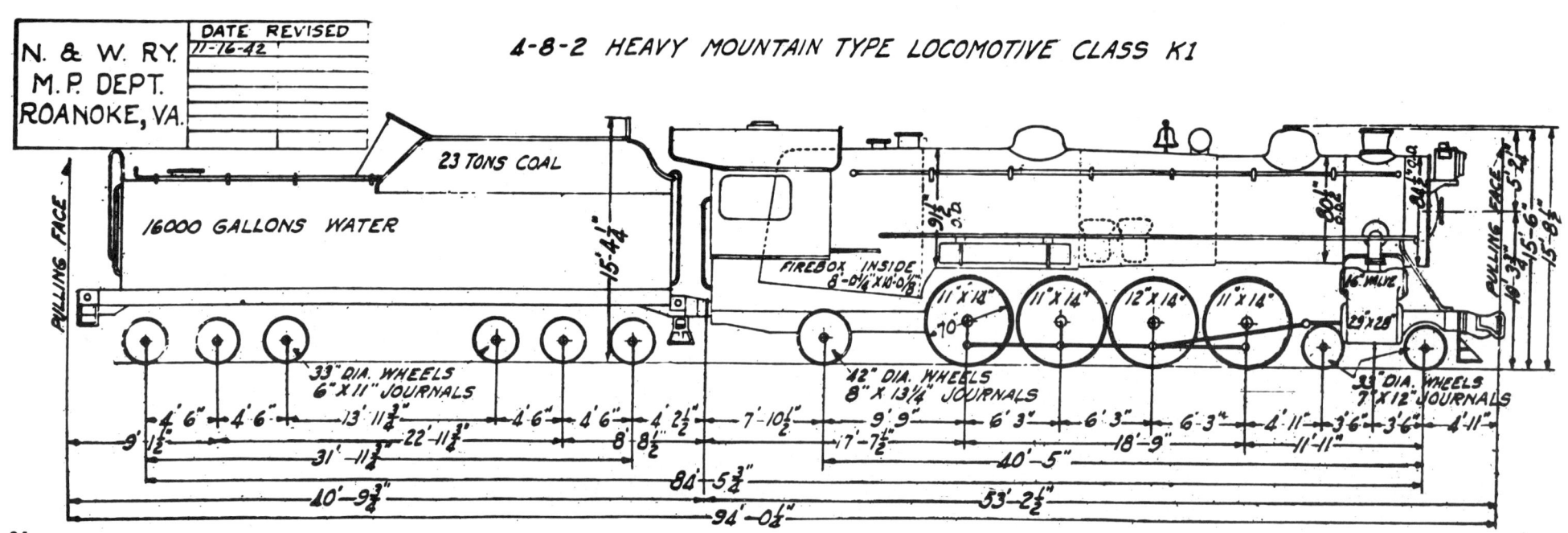

THE 1936 ROSTER:
100-107 (Roanoke Shops, 1916)
108-115 (Roanoke Shops, 1917)

| Driv. Diam. | Total Loco Weight | Weight On Drivers | Cylinders Bore x Stroke | Boiler Pressure | Tractive Effort |
|---|---|---|---|---|---|
| 70" | 347,000 lbs. | 236,000 lbs. | 29"x28" | 220 psi | 62,920 lbs. |

21

RIGHT: Marvin Cohen photographed K1 104 on the point of a healthy time freight at Radford, Virginia back in September, 1954.

BELOW: 113 idles between assignments at Crewe, Virginia, in the fall of 1958. Several K1's wound up with these ex-C&O tenders. *Collection of Harold K. Vollrath.*

# 4-8-2 K2

Specifications for the N&W's highly-regarded K2 Mountains were developed by committees of loco builders and railway mechanical officials working under the direction of the United States Railroad Administration during World War One. The U.S.R.A. had been formed to operate the nation's railroads in 1917 when some Eastern carriers proved unable to cope with the upsurge in port traffic brought on by our tardy entry into the conflict. While Federal operation of the railroads was a big mistake, the locomotives ordered by the administration to ease motive power shortages proved most popular. Believe it or not, plans for no less than twelve classes of locos were turned out in a little over two months.

The twelve U.S.R.A. types were 0-6-0, 0-8-0, 2-6-6-2, 2-8-8-2, and light and heavy varieties of 4-6-2, 4-8-2, 2-8-2, and 2-10-2. A total of 1,856 locos were built under the aegis of the U.S.R.A., and a further 3,251 steamers of essentially similar specifications were built between the return of the roads to private operation in 1919 and 1953. Of all the varieties, only the 2-6-6-2's were not re-ordered.

The N&W was allocated ten of the Heavy Mountains, built at an average cost of $67,900, and twelve copies were purchased four years later. (The N&W also received 50 2-8-8-2's — see class Y3).

| THE 1936 ROSTER:<br>116-125 (Brooks, 1919, for U.S.R.A.)<br>126-137 (Baldwin, 1923) | Driv.<br>Diam.<br>70"* | Total Loco<br>Weight<br>352,000 lbs. | Weight On<br>Drivers<br>243,000 lbs. | Cylinders<br>Bore x Stroke<br>28"x30" | Boiler<br>Pressure<br>220 psi | Tractive<br>Effort<br>63,932 lbs. |

*Increased from 69".

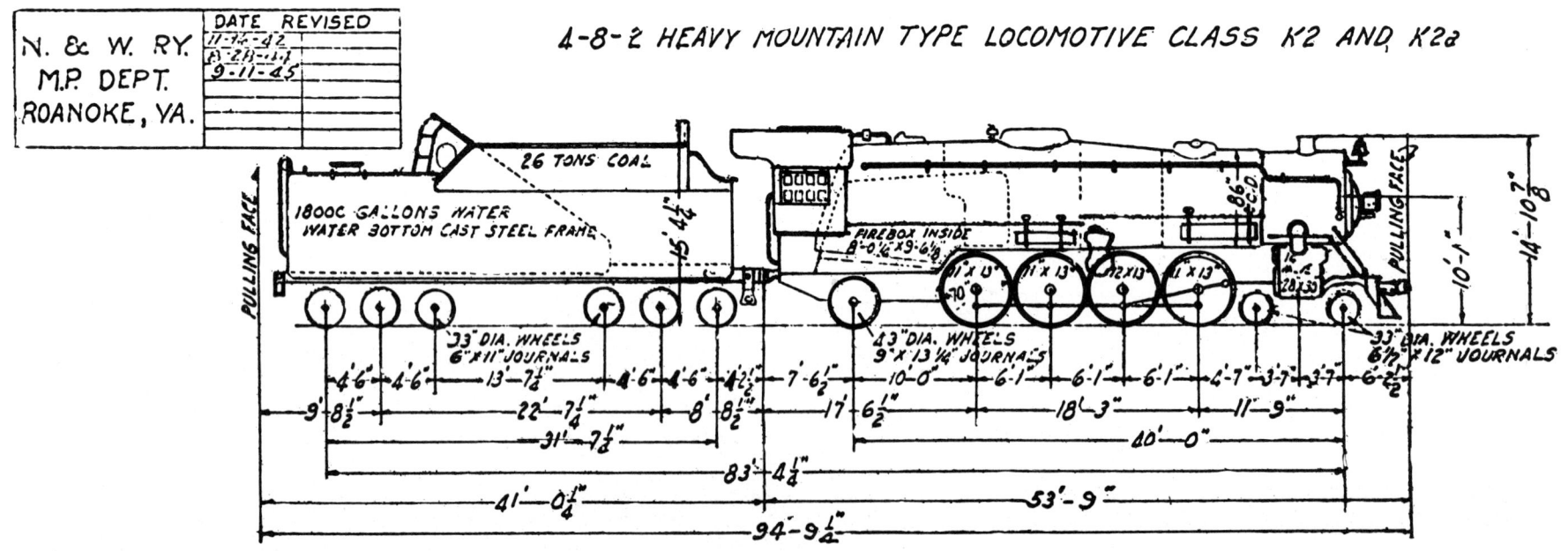

These photos of K2 124 (an original) and K2a 128 exemplify the look of this class during World War Two. Observe the inspection manholes, covered sanding valves peculiar to 124, and graphited boiler jacket in the photo below. (128 *from the Vollrath Collection*).

The class K2 locos underwent an amazing metamorphosis in Roanoke Shops in the late 'forties, and emerged as America's most elegant 4-8-2's. Their shroud was an abbreviated version of that designed in 1941 for the J-class 4-8-4's. The streamlining was deficient in only one respect — instead of an all-welded tank, the locos trailed riveted tenders quite like those built by Roanoke for class-A 2-6-6-4's and the later 2-8-8-2's.

LEFT: Sleek 116 at Norfolk, 5/56.
*Collection of Harold K. Vollrath.*

OPPOSITE: 137 pops off steam at Montvale, Virginia while awaiting the passage of a two-car passenger local in the charge of a sister K2. In September, 1957, a streamlined steamer on any sort of train was a precious find for photographer John Briggs.

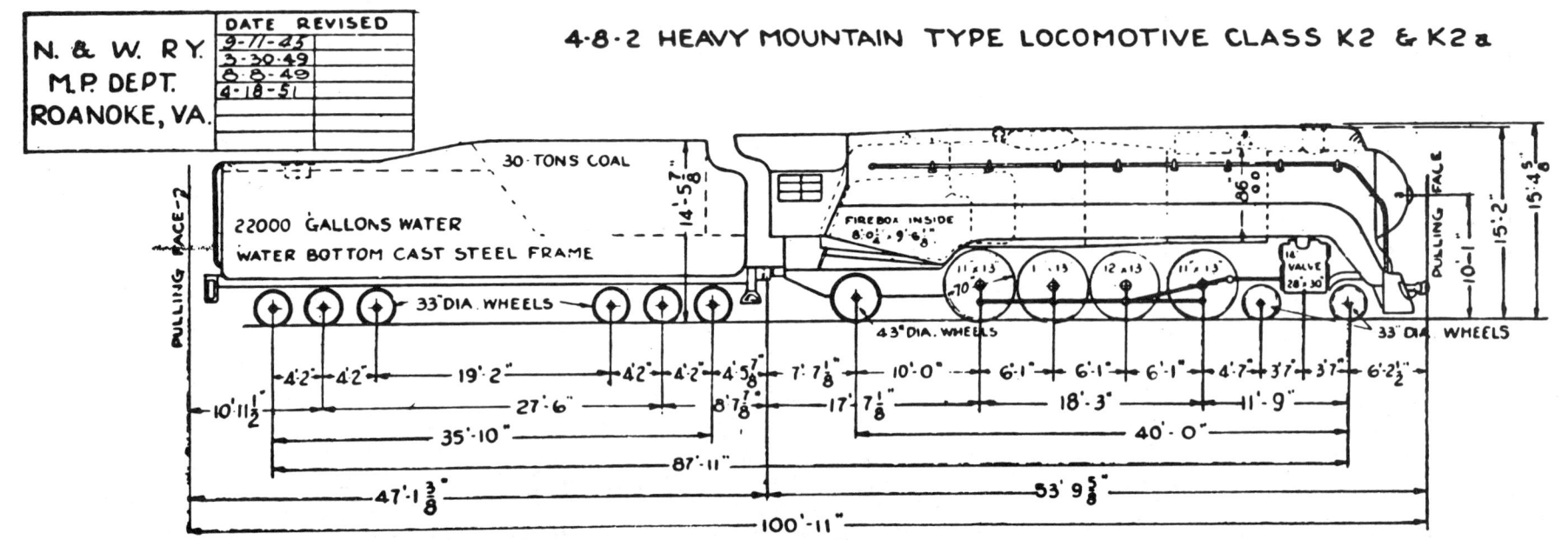

### A FLEETING GLIMPSE . . .

Colorful K2 114 pierces the monotony of a dreary fall day during the wane of steam passenger operation on the N&W. Sadly, such duties will soon be entrusted to leased Atlantic Coast Line and Richmond, Fredericksburg and Potomac E-unit diesels.

*Courtesy Don Ball, Jr.*

# 4-8-2 K3

The K3 4-8-2's were one of the N&W's few motive power mistakes. They were among the heaviest Mountains ever built, and their bulk restricted them to mainline track. Their small wheels resulted in very high starting tractive effort, but made the K3's difficult to balance and hard on the track at any speed above 35 m.p.h. The overweight and unloved locos were sold during the war to the D&RGW, RF&P, and W&LE. *Photo, Harold Vollrath collection.*

THE 1936 ROSTER:
200-209 (Roanoke Shops, 1926)

| Driv. Diam. | Total Loco Weight | Weight On Drivers | Cylinders Bore x Stroke | Boiler Pressure | Tractive Effort |
|---|---|---|---|---|---|
| 63" | 401,900 lbs. | 275,400 lbs. | 28"x30" | 225 psi | 68,880 lbs. |

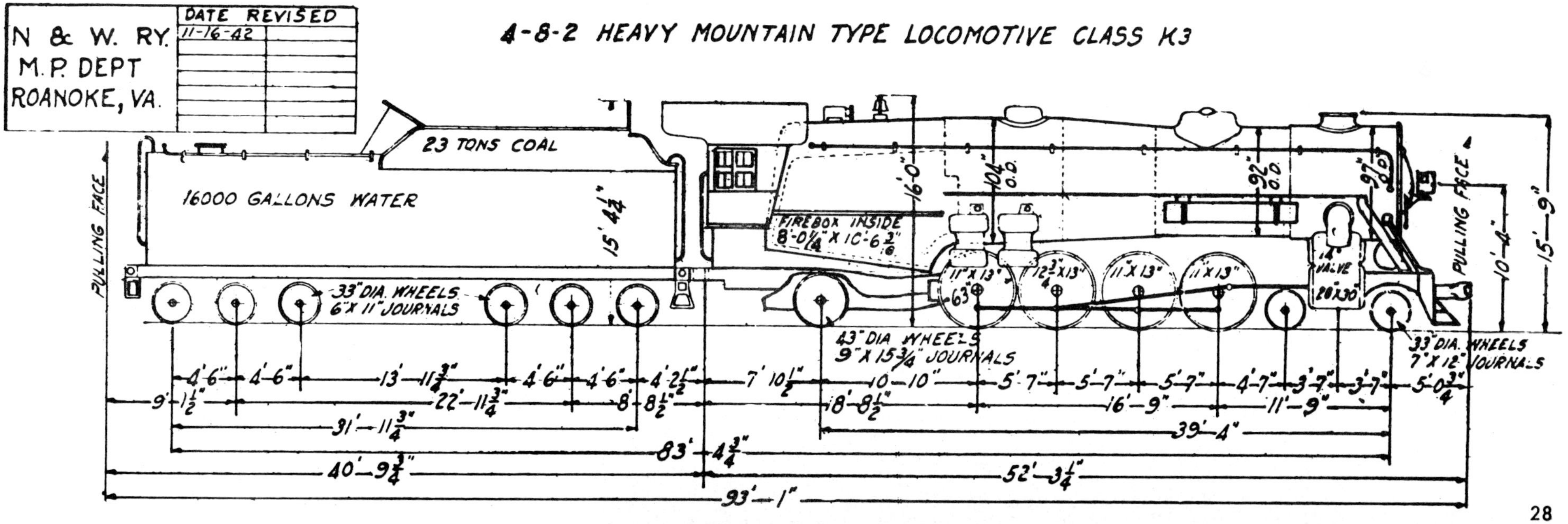

# 2-6-6-2 Z1

The thrifty Mallet Compounds used their steam twice. Steam was first admitted from the boiler at full pressure into the cylinders driving the rear engine, and then exhausted into the mammoth low-pressure cylinders on the articulated front engine. The Z1a's like 1345 at right had old-time slide valve chests up front, with more modern piston-valve cylinders in the rear.

THE 1936 ROSTER:
1315-1324, 1326, 1328-1339 (Richmond, 1912), 1341, 1342, 1344-1349, 1351, 1352, 1354-1359, 1361-1365, 1367, 1368, 1370, 1371, 1373-1379 (Baldwin, 1913), 1380-1387, 1389-1398, 1400-1419 (Baldwin, 1914), 1420-1429 (Schenectady, 1915), 1431, 1434, 1435, 1438, 1440-1459 (Schenectady, 1916), 1460, 1461, 1463-1465, 1467 (Schenectady, 1917), 1470-1489 (Schenectady, 1918)

| Driv. Diam. | Total Loco Weight | Weight On Drivers | Cylinders Bore x Stroke | Boiler Pressure | Tractive Effort Simple | Compound |
|---|---|---|---|---|---|---|
| 56½" | 427,000 to 440,000 lbs. | 354,500 to 376,581 lbs. | 35"x32" front 22"x32" rear | 225 psi | 90,996 lbs. | 75,830 lbs. |

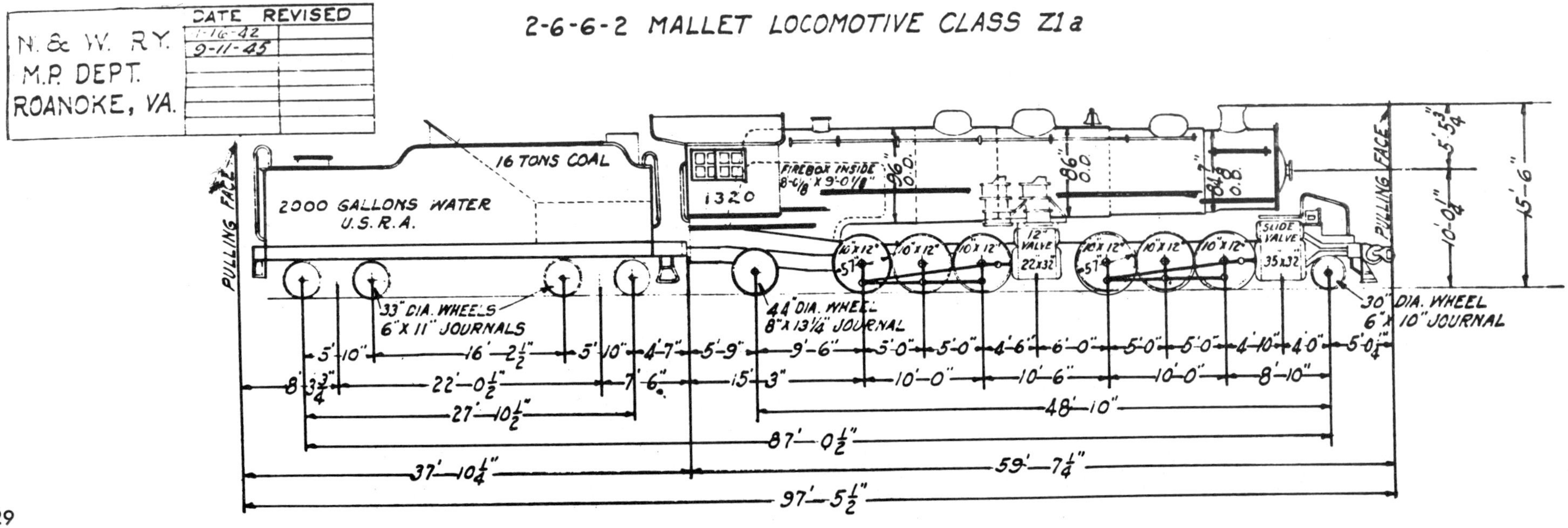

2-6-6-2 MALLET LOCOMOTIVE CLASS Z1a

Z1a 1321 was caught in this perfect exposure at the Cincinnati engine terminal on a clear September day in 1938. The camera's optics, the fine-grain film, the illumination, and the light coat of dust on the engine have worked together to reveal even the slightest imperfections in the loco's finish. This loco has received a U.S.R.A. tender from a Y3 2-8-8-2.

The Z1b's were best distinguished from the Z1a's by the more modern front cylinders, but the Worthington feedwater heater on the left balanced by the two cross-compound air pumps opposite was also a dependable clue. The two subclasses drew mine runs and heavy switching duty, hence both footboards and marker lights. *Two photos, collection of Harold K. Vollrath.*

What words best describe this Don Ball shot of Z1b 1476? We suggest BRUTE FORCE!

# 2-8-8-2 Y2

Though the U.S.R.A. ordered a halt to production of custom steam loco designs in 1918, many locomotives already under construction were completed to ease the motive power shortage. The first twenty-three Y2's were finished under these terms, and eight more were built by Roanoke after restrictions were eased. While lighter than the U.S.R.A. 2-8-8-2's, the Y2's received a slightly higher tractive effort rating when working at the same boiler pressure.

THE 1936 ROSTER:
1700, 1701 (Roanoke Shops, 1918)
1702 (Roanoke Shops, 1919)
1703-1704 (Roanoke Shops, 1921)
1705-1710 (Roanoke Shops, 1924)
1711-1730 (Baldwin, 1919)

| Driv. Diam. | Total Loco Weight | Weight On Drivers | Cylinders Bore x Stroke | Boiler Pressure | Tractive Effort Simple | Compound |
|---|---|---|---|---|---|---|
| 56" | 526,000 lbs. | 472,000 lbs. | 39"x32" front 25"x32" rear | 240 to 270 psi | 123,960 to 158,894 lbs. | 103,300 to 138,000 lbs. |

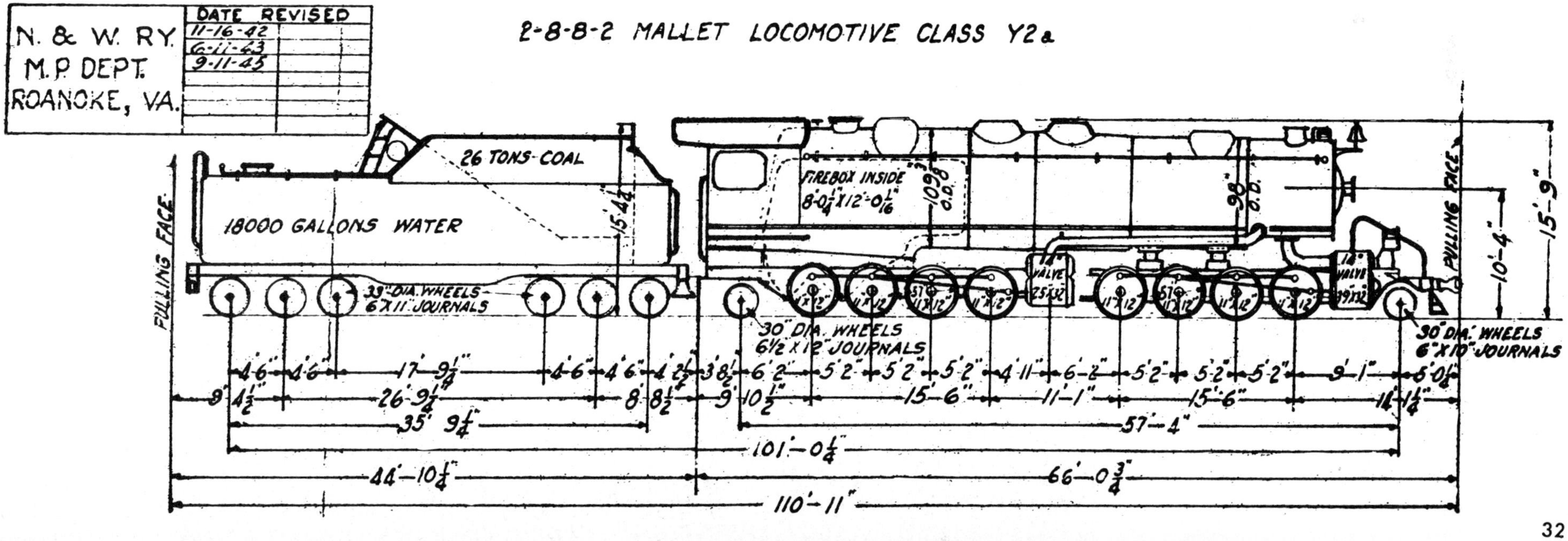

About 1930, Y2's 1702, 1706, and 1714 were fitted with two Franklin tender boosters in a further attempt to increase tractive effort. The boosters only operated up to a speed of about 15 m.p.h., and the results were directly proportional to the weight of fuel and water remaining in the tender. We don't know how long the trial lasted. (Locos 1700 and 1711 were likewise fitted with Bethlehem boosters). *N&W photo.*

# 2-8-8-2 Y3

The 50 U.S.R.A. 2-8-8-2's proved well-suited for mineral freight service, and the N&W ordered 30 identical locos in 1923 — the Y3a's. Indeed, the railway looked no further for a compound mallet design, and the N&W built or bought no less than 110 essentially similar machines in classes Y4, Y5, Y6, Y6a, and Y6b between 1927 and 1952. RIGHT: Y3a 2068. *Collection of Harold K. Vollrath.*

**THE 1936 ROSTER:**
Y3 class (Built for U.S.R.A.)
2000-2044 (Schenectady, 1919)
2045-2049 (Baldwin, 1919)
Y3a class (Built for N&W)
2050-2079 (Richmond, 1923)

| Driv. Diam. | Total Loco Weight | Weight On Drivers | Cylinders Bore x Stroke | Boiler Pressure | Tractive Effort Simple | Tractive Effort Compound |
|---|---|---|---|---|---|---|
| 57" | 539,000 lbs. | 485,000 lbs. | 39"x32" front 25"x32" rear | 270 psi | 136,985 lbs. | 114,154 lbs. |

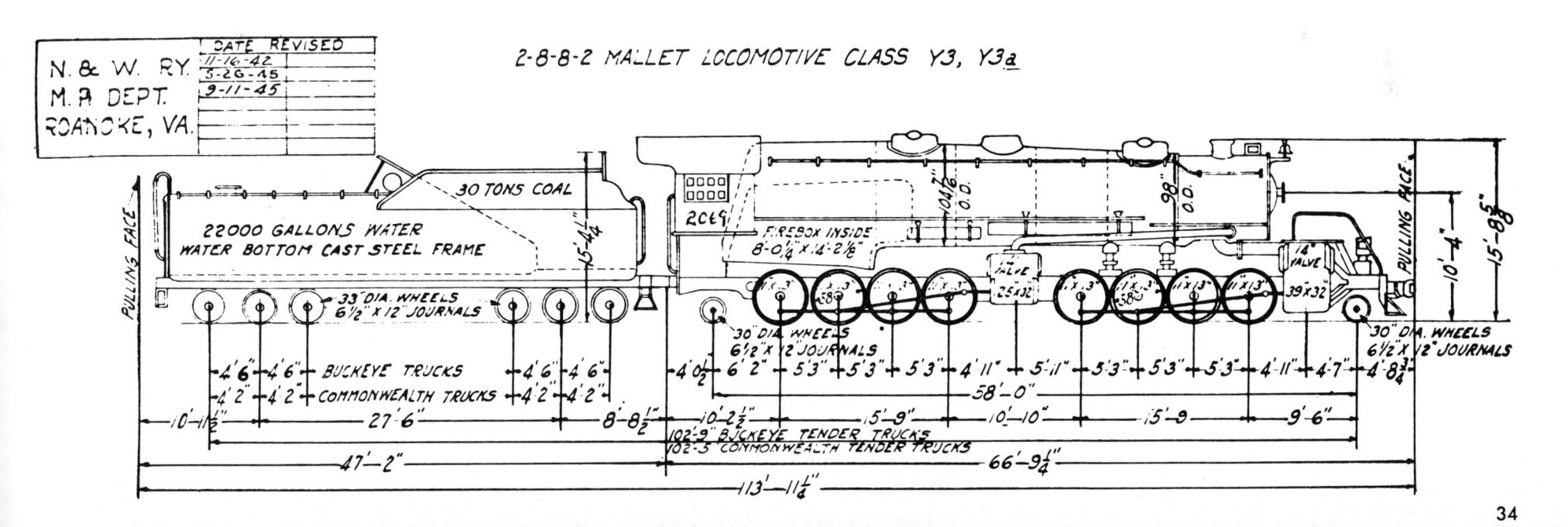

34

The 2023, an original U.S.R.A. 2-8-8-2, makes ready to back onto a gravel extra at Bluefield in the summer of 1958. The footboard pilot was a definite clue that this loco was seldom assigned to mainline freights at this late date. *Marvin H. Cohen photo.*

Y3a 2069 may never have returned to service after she was photographed stored with her stack capped at Shaffers Crossing in May, 1958. This type of boiler-tube pilot was standard for Norfolk and Western 2-8-8-2's drawing regular road duty.

# 2-8-8-2 Y4

One question naturally comes up when looking at a photo of an N&W 2-8-8-2: What class is it? Well, the Y2's were unique, but the Y3's and Y3a's can only be differentiated by number. The Y4's were the oldest 2-8-8-2's on the railway which were fitted with slant-front cabs, but they were often confused with Y5's and Y6's. Five Y4's had tenders with four-axle trucks, unique to this class on the N&W. However, the other Y4's were best spotted by reference to the loco number.

LEFT: 2083 under steam at Roanoke, 1954. *C. W. Jernstrom.*

| THE 1936 ROSTER: | Driv. Diam. | Total Loco Weight | Weight On Drivers | Cylinders Bore x Stroke | Boiler Pressure | Tractive Effort Simple / Compound |
|---|---|---|---|---|---|---|
| 2080-2089 (Richmond, 1927) | 58" | 567,000 lbs. | 508,500 lbs. | 39"x32" front 25"x32" rear | 270 psi | 136,985 lbs. / 114,154 lbs. |

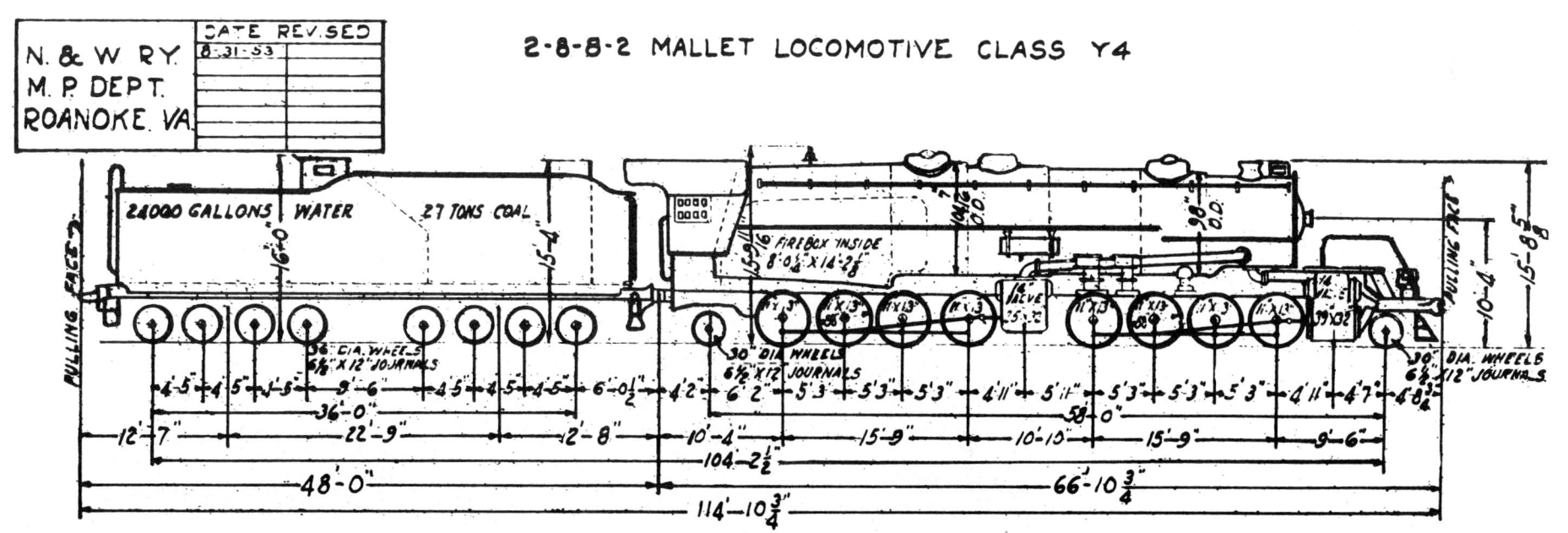

The photo at the left shows Y4 2089 at Bluefield in 1947, still trailing an older-style tender. The view below from the Harold Vollrath collection shows sister 2081 a little over a year later. Some of this class eventually received eight-axle tenders from ACL 4-8-4's. Note the double-decker air reservoirs on the 2081, and the two-cylinder stoker engine poking out from under the cab of the 2089.

# 2-8-8-2 Y5

The Y5's were the last N&W steamers built with friction bearings and fabricated engine beds. Six years later, Roanoke turned out the first of the Y6's — locos built to the same dimensions, but with cast steel frames, roller bearings on all ten engine axles, and more sophisticated mechanical lubrication. The Y6 locos cost more to build, but the initial expense was easily offset by greater availability and much lower maintenance costs. Accordingly, the Y5's went back to Roanoke in 1940 and received cast frames, roller bearings, and all other refinements necessary to bring the veterans up to Y6 standards. LEFT: 2093 before modernization.

**THE 1936 ROSTER:**
2090-2099 (Roanoke Shops, 1930)
2100-2108 (Roanoke Shops, 1931)
2109 (Roanoke Shops, 1932)

| Driv. Diam. | Total Loco Weight | Weight On Drivers | Cylinders Bore x Stroke | Boiler Pressure | Tractive Effort Simple / Compound |
|---|---|---|---|---|---|
| 58" | 582,900 lbs. | 522,850 lbs. | 39"x32" front 25"x32" rear | 300 psi | 152,206 lbs. / 126,838 lbs. |

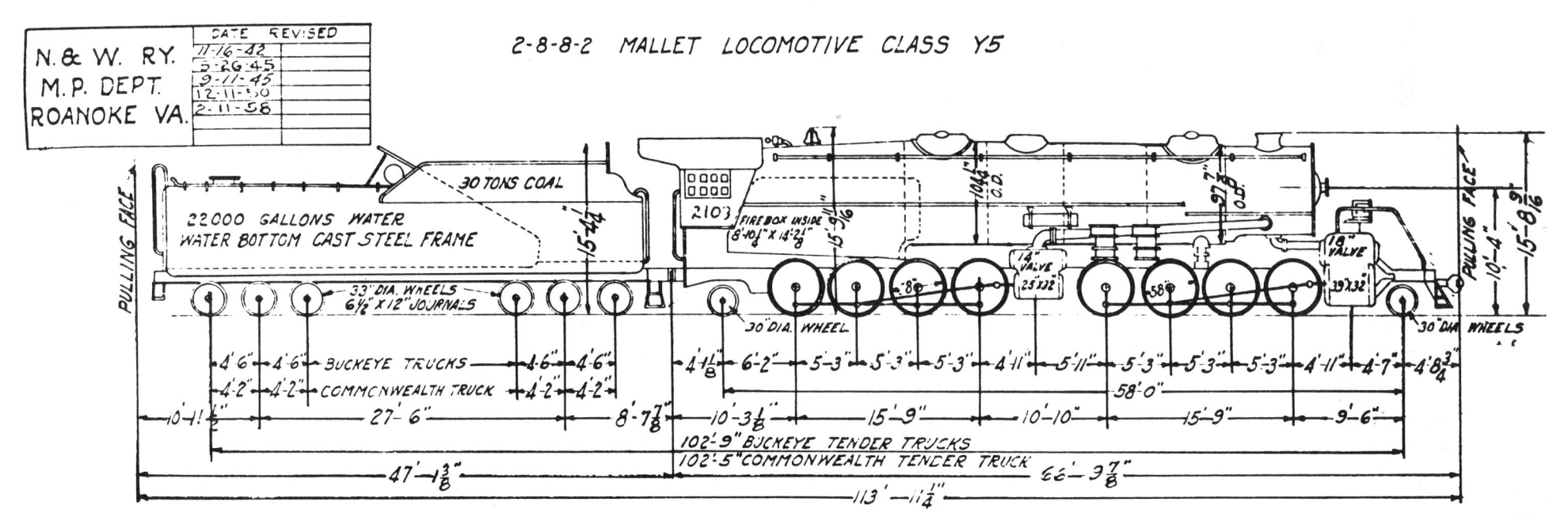

38

Frank Zahn found Y5 2109 proceeding through Roanoke on the point of a freight in March, 1959. This perspective gives modellers a good look at what goes where atop that massive boiler.

After rebuilding, the Y5 class retained inboard bearings on the lead and trailing trucks, and that is a safe way to differentiate the group from the Y6's. Shown here at Roanoke in 1954, 2112 was fitted with unusual large sand domes.
*Collection of Harold K. Vollrath.*

When rebuilt, the Y5's went through a complicated renumbering. 2101-2109 retained their old numbers, and here are the old/new numbers for the rest:

| | | | | |
|---|---|---|---|---|
| 2094/2110 | 2090/2111 | 2098/2112 | 2096/2113 | 2095/2114 |
| 2100/2115 | 2091/2116 | 2097/2117 | 2099/2118 | 2093/2119 |

Locomotive 2092 was destroyed in 1937, and never rebuilt.

# Part 2: Modern Power

A new era in motive power began when the first class A 2-6-6-4 steamed forth from Roanoke Shops in May, 1936. Loco 1200 was a high-wheeled simple articulated designed for high-speed performance on either freight or passenger trains. She was the first N&W loco with roller bearings on all axles, she was capable of sustained speeds in excess of 70 miles per hour, and she exerted a sustained drawbar horsepower of 6,300 at 45 m.p.h. — more "pull-power" than *five* of the most powerful diesels then available. The receipt of Y6 2120 in September of that year meant vast improvements in the transit of tonnage freights over the hillier central parts of the system. Delivery of J 600 in October, 1941 gave the railway a powerful passenger locomotive capable of speeds over 100 m.p.h., but sure-footed enough to keep any normal passenger consist on time over the roller-coaster profile of the N&W main.

The new locos came at a fortuitous time. Shortly, the N&W's resources were once more severely strained by a world conflict. The members of the A and Y6 classes comprised only one-third of the locos assigned to road freight service, yet by 1945 their high availability enabled them to account for 68% of the system's total freight mileage. When traffic slacked off after the war, the newer locos did even more work, since the uneconomical older steeds were at last sent out to pasture. By 1953, the 14 J's handled 84% of the N&W's passenger train-miles, and the 43 A's, 19 modernized Y5's, and 80 Y6's teamed up to lug 94% of the line's freight ton-miles.

The new era ended in early 1960, when several steamers on the property were still shy of their eighth birthday. What brought the era to an end was surely not a lack of faith, but rather unavoidable reliance on several suppliers of steam locomotive "specialties" who found the N&W's needs insufficient inducement to stay in business.

RIGHT: Frank Zahn found Y6a 2160 assisting the A in charge of an eastbound coal train at Blue Ridge, Va. in July, 1958. In contemporary railroading, what sight compares?

42

## ROSTER RECAPITULATION MODERN LOCOMOTIVES:

| CLASS | TYPE | 1936 | 1942 | 1944 | 1949 | 1953 | 1954 | 1956 | 1961 | All-time Total |
|---|---|---|---|---|---|---|---|---|---|---|
| A | 2-6-6-4 | 2 | 10 | 35 | 40 | 43 | 43 | 43 | 1 | 43 |
| J | 4-8-4 | 0 | 5 | 11 | 11 | 14 | 14 | 14 | 1 | 14 |
| S1 | 0-8-0 | 0 | 0 | 0 | 0 | 30 | 30 | 30 | 0 | 30 |
| S1a | 0-8-0 | 0 | 0 | 0 | 0 | 45 | 45 | 45 | 6 | 45 |
| TE1 | C-C+C-C | 0 | 0 | 0 | 0 | 0 | 1 | 1 | 0 | 1 |
| Y6 | 2-8-8-2 | 5 | 35 | 35 | 35 | 35 | 35 | 35 | 15 | 35 |
| Y6a | 2-8-8-2 | 0 | 5 | 15 | 15 | 15 | 15 | 15 | 3 | 15 |
| Y6b | 2-8-8-2 | 0 | 0 | 0 | 17 | 30 | 30 | 30 | 16 | 30 |
| ALL | | 7 | 55 | 96 | 118 | 212 | 213 | 213 | 42 | 213 |

### PRESERVED TODAY ON PUBLIC DISPLAY:

Y6a 2156 at the National Museum of Transport, St. Louis, Mo., and the two subjects of Howard Fogg's painting on our cover, J 611 and A 1218 at the Roanoke Transportation Museum.

### MODERNIZATION ON THE BALANCE SHEET: MAINTENANCE COSTS COMPARED

The table reproduced below was published in March, 1945 in a publicity booklet entitled *Modern Coal-Burning Steam Locomotives of the Norfolk and Western Railway Company.*

#### PASSENGER LOCOMOTIVES

| | Class J Modern 4-8-4 | Class K2 Conventional 4-8-2 | Percent Difference Modern Compared With Conventional Design |
|---|---|---|---|
| Tractive Power (Pounds) | 73,300 | 63,800 | 14.9 more |
| Maintenance Cost per 100 Locomotive Miles | $11.54 | $15.69 | 26.4 less |
| Maintenance Cost per Million Tractive Power Pound Miles | $ 1.57 | $ 2.46 | 36.2 less |

#### FREIGHT AND HEAVY PASSENGER LOCOMOTIVES

| | Class A Modern 2-6-6-4 | Class K3 Conventional 4-8-2 | Percent Difference Modern Compared With Conventional Design |
|---|---|---|---|
| Tractive Power (Pounds) | 114,000 | 68,880 | 65.5 more |
| Maintenance Cost per 100 Locomotive Miles | $21.12 | $21.25 | .6 less |
| Maintenance Cost per Million Tractive Power Pound Miles | $ 2.02 | $ 3.08 | 34.4 less |

#### HEAVY FREIGHT LOCOMOTIVES

| | Class Y6 Modern 2-8-8-2 | Class Y5 Conventional 2-8-8-2 | Percent Difference Modern Compared With Conventional Design |
|---|---|---|---|
| Tractive Power (Pounds) Simple / Compound | 152,206 / 126,838 | 152,206 / 126,838 | ........ / ........ |
| Maintenance Cost per 100 Locomotive Miles | $23.76 | $37.79 | 37.1 less |
| Maintenance Cost per Million Tractive Power Pound Miles | $ 1.87 | $ 2.98 | 37.2 less |

**TWO A'S DEMONSTRATE THE MEANING OF ARTICULATION:**
1222 and 1234 on the ready track at Columbus, Ohio in April, 1958.
*From the collection of C. W. Jernstrom.*

# 2-6-6-4
# A

Fittingly, the first letter of the alphabet was selected to designate the N&W 2-6-6-4's of 1936. Five S.A.L. locos of similar wheel arrangement had been the inspiration for the A's, but the new locos overwhelmed them by any measure. No Yellowstone (2-8-8-4) could run so fast, no Challenger (4-6-6-4) was as powerful, and the nearest competition, the Allegheny (2-6-6-6) types of the C&O and Virginian were five years in the future, and only enjoyed the advantage of greater steaming capacity, attended by an enormous increase in locomotive weight.

RIGHT: Millions viewed 1206 on display at the New York World's Fair in 1940. A's through 1209 had Laird crossheads.

| Road Numbers and Years Built by Roanoke Shops: | Driv. Diam. | Total Loco Weight | Weight On Drivers | Cylinders Bore x Stroke | Boiler Pressure | Tractive Effort (Simple) |
|---|---|---|---|---|---|---|
| 1200, 1201 (1936), 1202-1209 (1937), 1210-1224 (1943) | 70" | 570,000 lbs. | 430,100 lbs. | 24"x30" | 275 psi* | 104,500 lbs. |
| 1225-1234 (1944), 1235-1239 (1949), 1240-1243 (1950) | 70" | 573,100 lbs. | 432,350 lbs. | 24"x30" | 300 psi | 114,000 lbs. |

* Later increased to 300 psi.

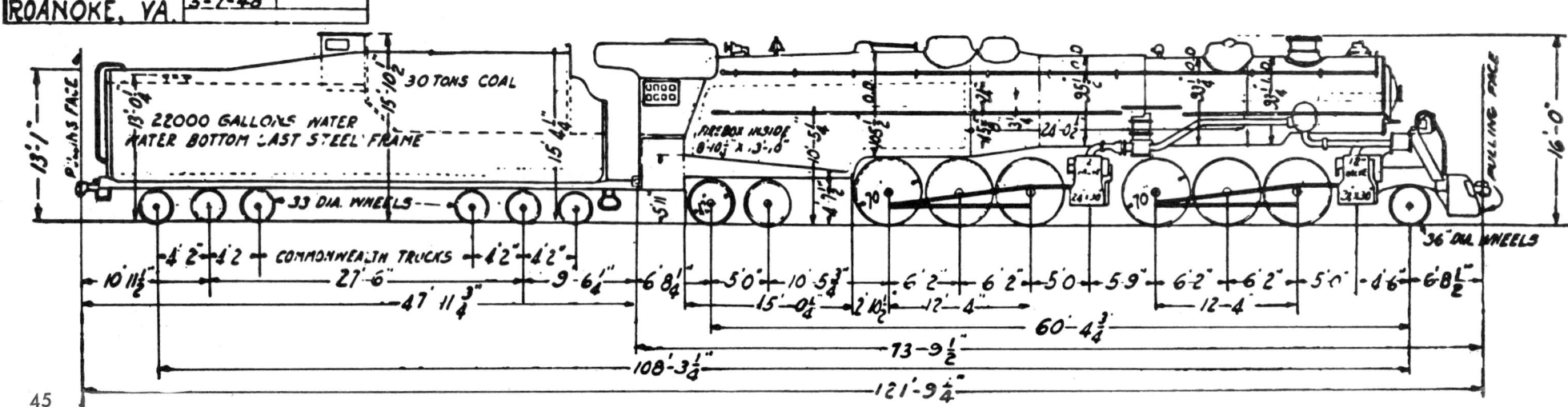

This John Briggs photo of the 1212 shows the fabricated smooth pilot usually associated with the A's. Note the feedwater heater sunken into the smokebox top, and the mounting of the two Westinghouse air pumps — one on each side, opposite one another for balance.

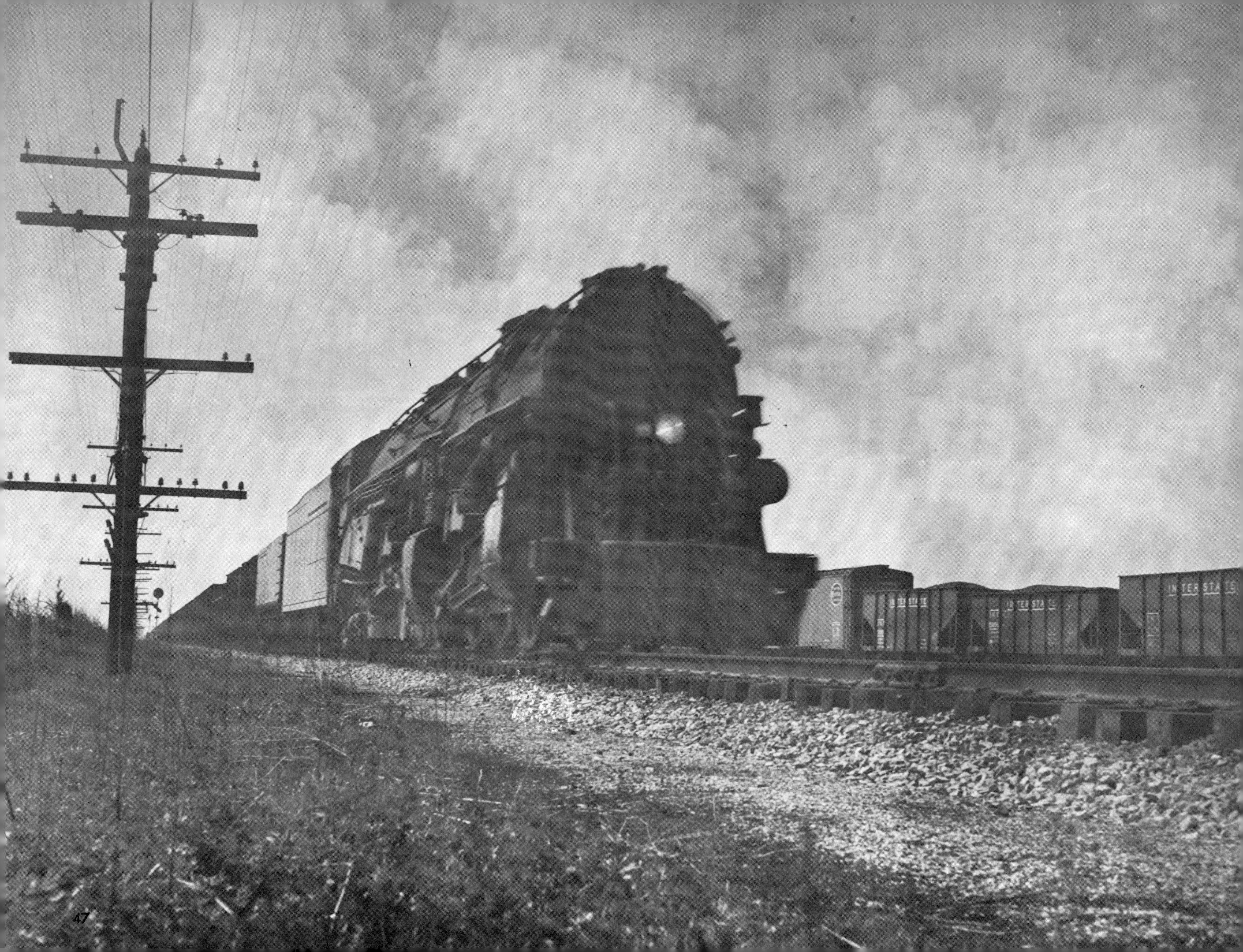
INTERSTATE
INTERSTATE

A IN MOTION

This dynamic photo by Don Ball, Jr., shows a speeding A on the point of a seemingly limitless string of empty coal hoppers.

A AT REST

In July, 1959 Karl R. Zimmermann came upon the 1234 snoozing between assignments at Shaffers Crossing roundhouse.

## ATMOSPHERIC CONTRASTS

On a brilliant day in July, 1957, Bill Jernstrom found class A 1226 sweeping through Vinton, Virginia, trailing an auxiliary water tender and a healthy manifest freight.

Sister 1224 strides along the Tug River Valley with 14,500 tons of westbound coal in tow. Thankfully, photographer Don Ball, Jr. was undeterred by the typically dreary weather on this day in February, 1958.

John Briggs found A 1238 struggling for footing while starting a mineral drag uphill on rain-slickened rail at Blue Ridge, Virginia. After much sanding and slipping, the effort succeeded, and several minutes later . . .

John's viewfinder framed the cabin car with conductor reaching out to receive train orders from the operator as the consist was urged onward by a second straining steamer, an unidentified Y6a.

# 2-8-8-2 Y6

Many roads wanted to dieselize their road freight operations during World War II, but were denied permission to order EMD FT's by the War Production Board. The N&W had no such urge, and accomplished the aims of dieselization with more modern steam locos of their own design and making. The 15 further Y6a's, plus their immediate predecessors, the Y5 and Y6 locos achieved utilization records equivalent to diesels in similar service assignments, thanks to their intrinsically sound design, and the N&W's remarkably efficient service facilities.

ROAD NUMBERS AND YEARS BUILT BY ROANOKE SHOPS:
Y6 class
2120-2123 (1936), 2125, 2126 (1937), 2127-2134 (1938), 2135-2143 (1939), 2144-2154 (1940)
Y6a class
2155-2170 (1942)
Y6b class
2171-2179 (1948), 2180-2187 (1949), 2188-2193 (1950), 2194-2196 (1951), 2197-2200 (1952)

| Driv. Diam. | Total Loco Weight | Weight On Drivers | Cylinders Bore x Stroke | Boiler Pressure | Tractive Effort Simple / Compound |
|---|---|---|---|---|---|
| 58" | 582,900 lbs. | 522,850 lbs. | 39"x32" front 25"x32" rear | 300 psi | 152,206 lbs. / 126,838 lbs. |

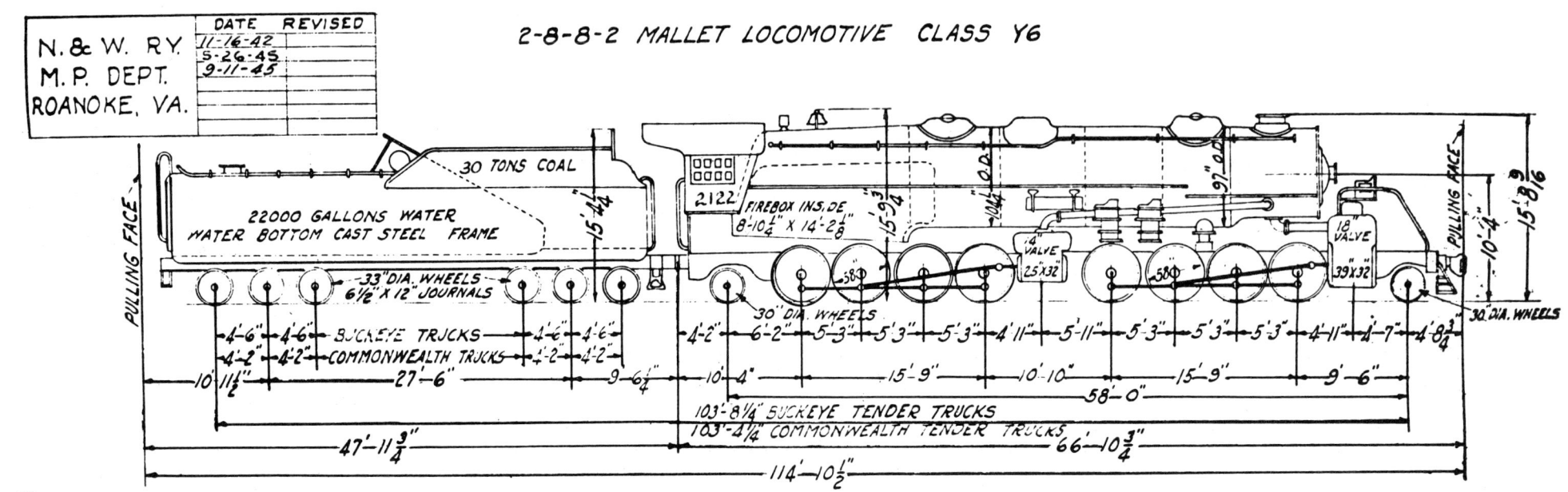

# 2-8-8-2 Y6a

FINAL ARTICULATED QUIZ QUESTION: How can you differentiate the Y6, Y6a and Y6b? ANSWER: The Y6b had the feed-water heater recessed in the smokebox, while classes Y6 and Y6a both had the older BL feedwater heater on the left, and two air pumps on the right. However, the Y6 and Y6a locos were so similar in later years that the engine number was the only certain clue.

This fine photo from Bill Jernstrom shows Y6a 2157 at Hagerstown in May, 1947. The open-ended box under the tender is a rack for rerailing frogs.

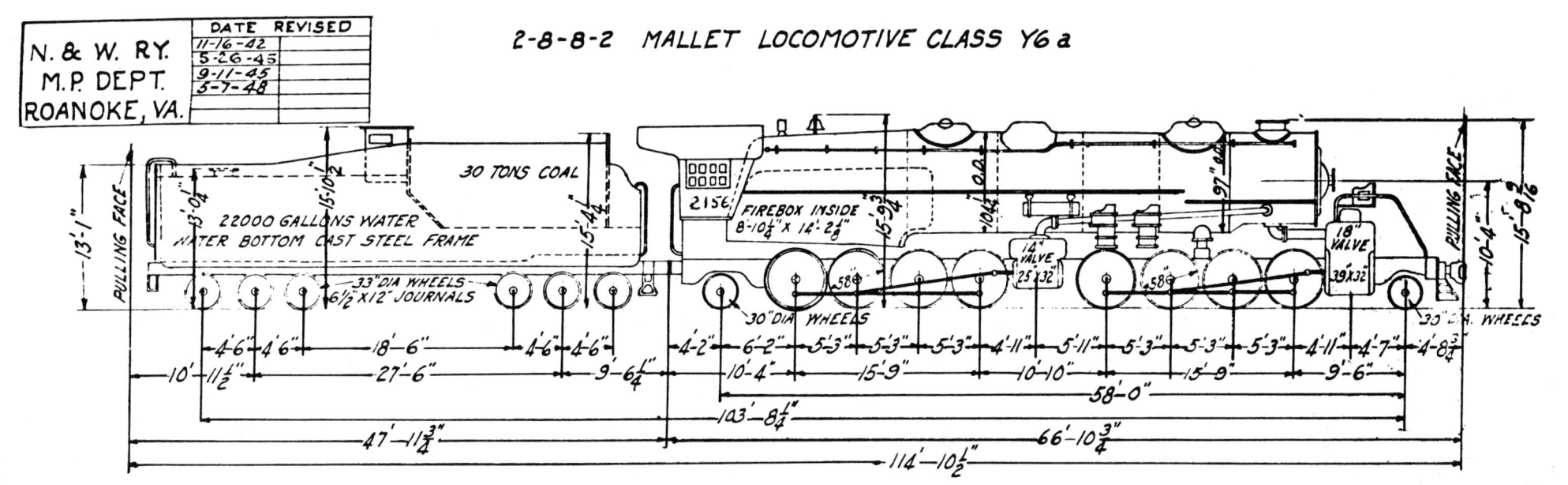

54

# 2-8-8-2 Y6b

# Apotheosis of the 2-8-8-2

The scale drawings on these five pages are, to our knowledge, the most detailed loco modellers' plans ever published. These views are a composite of an N&W model builder's general arrangement drawing and a more thorough set of plans which appeared in *Railroad Magazine* between March and June, 1950.

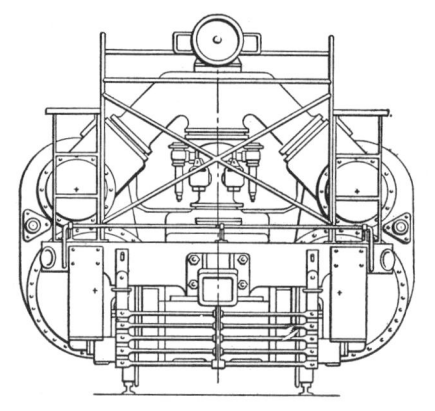

Front elevation of forward engine presents unusually massive appearance

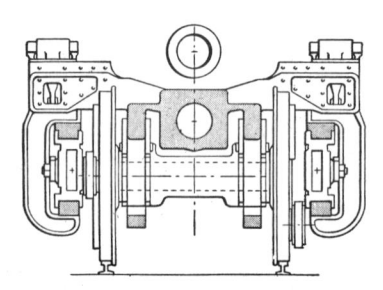

View at crosshead guide yoke. Return pipe cross-section at top

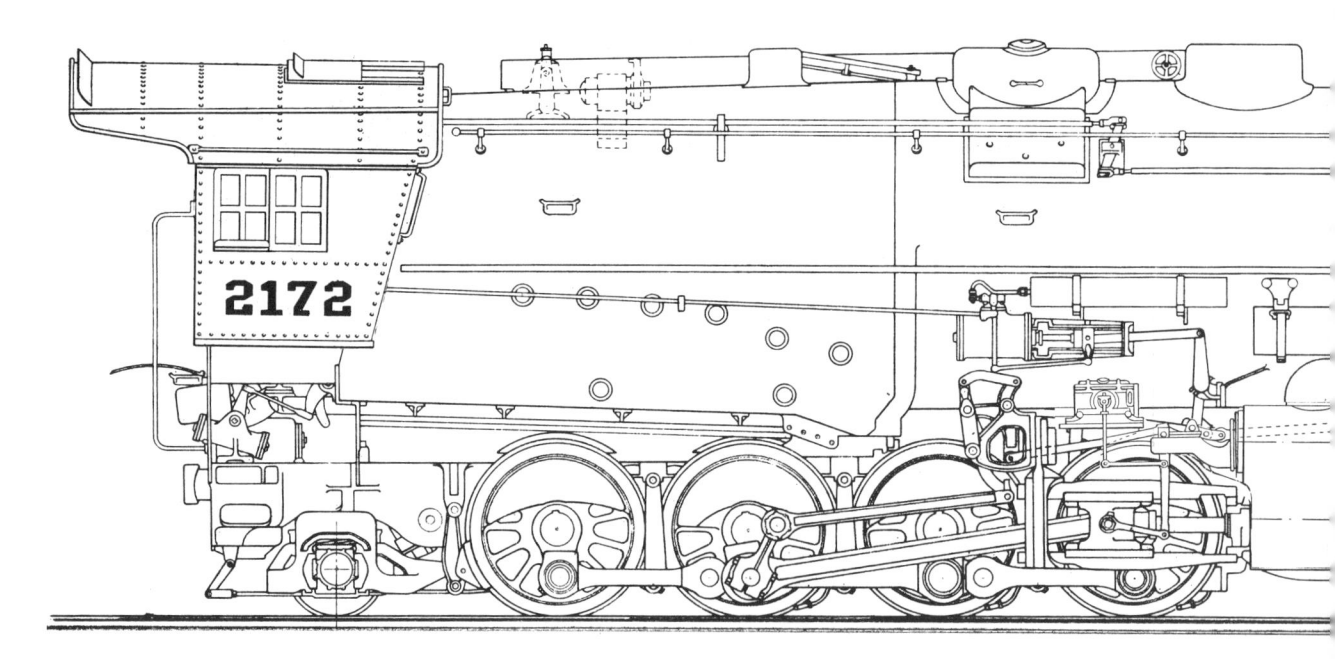

BELOW: These side views of the frames show the equalization rigging and the joint between front and rear engines.

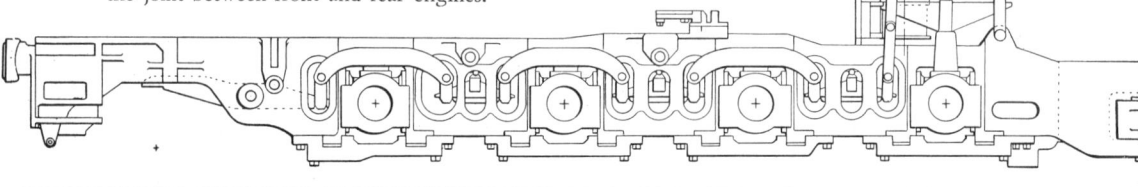

Plans are full
size for S gauge.
Scale: 3/16" = 1'0"

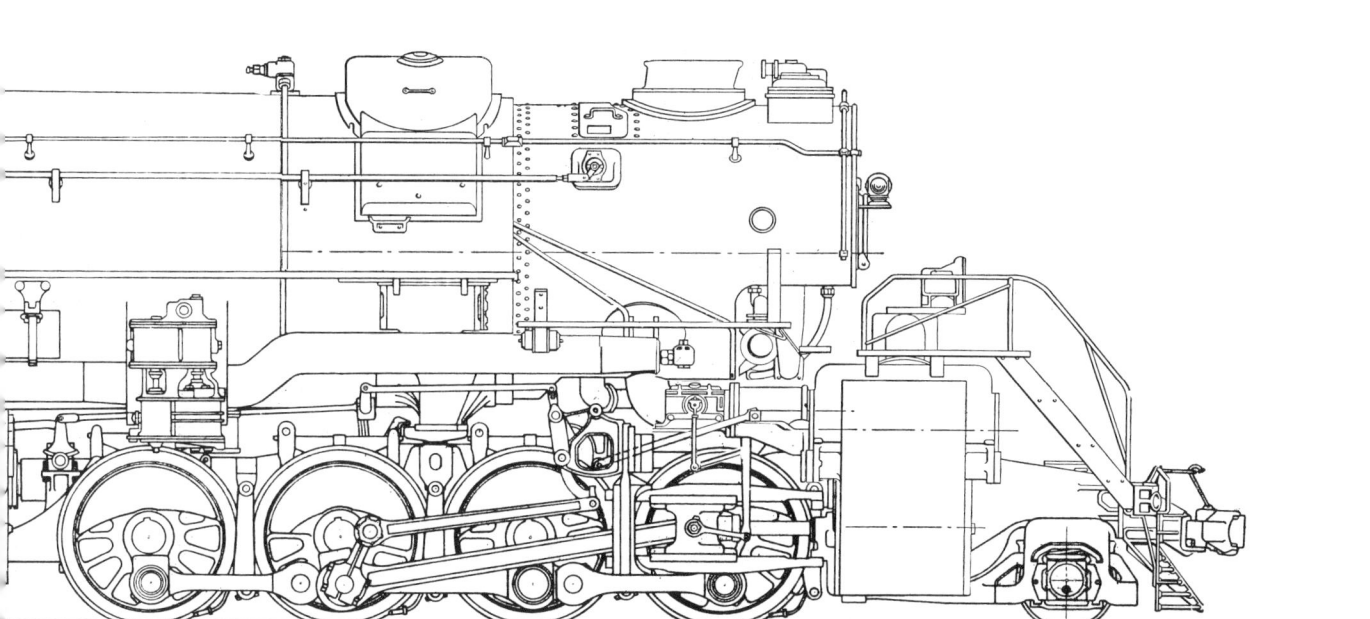

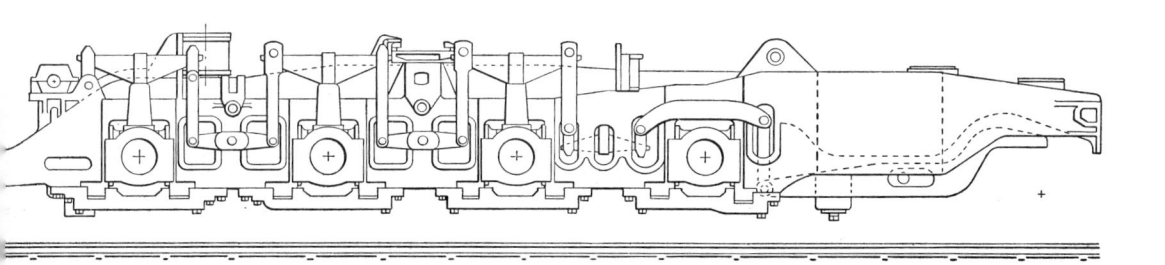

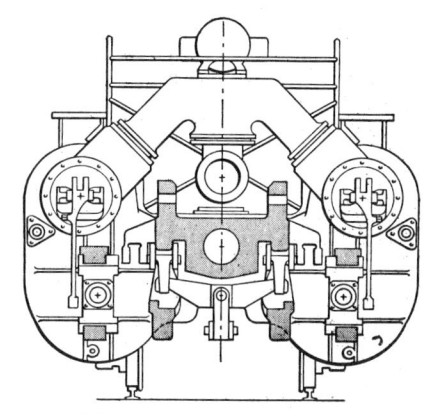

*Cylinders from rear, showing crosshead guides and combination levers*

*Below:* Section through crossheads

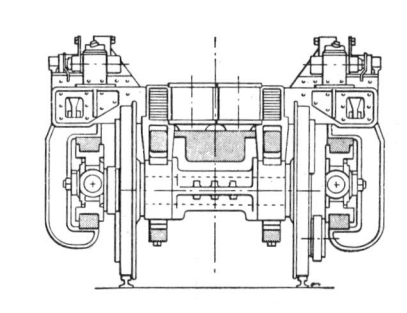

*Below:* Cross-section at No. 6 drivers

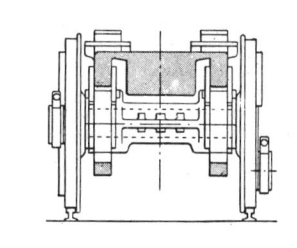

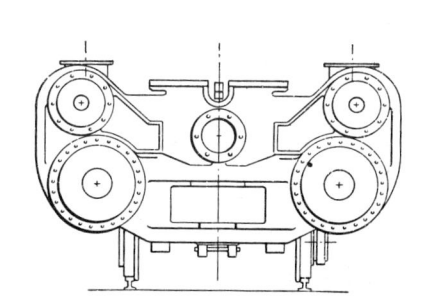

*Above:* Front view of rear engine

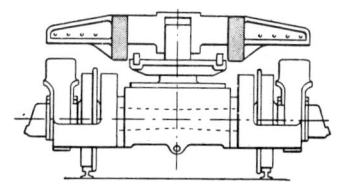

*Above:* Section at trailer truck

56

# 2-8-8-2 Y6b

ABOVE: N&W builder's photo of Y6b 2197 shot when new at Roanoke Shops, January, 1952.

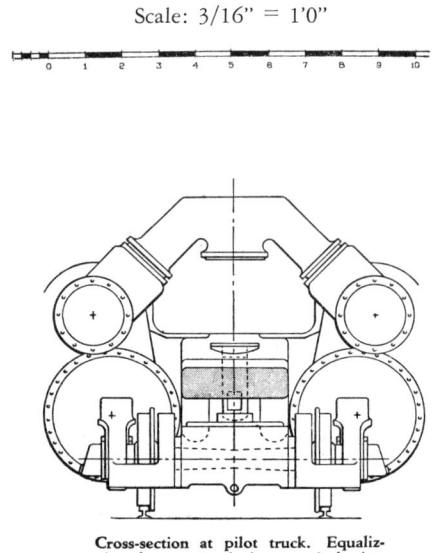

Scale: 3/16" = 1'0"

**Cross-section at pilot truck.** Equalizing lever extends into vertical pin

**Section at smokebox front,** showing placement of feedwater heater, classification lamps, hinged smokebox door, number plate, running boards and grab irons. Steam return-pipe wishbone and pressure-relief-valve dome are superimposed

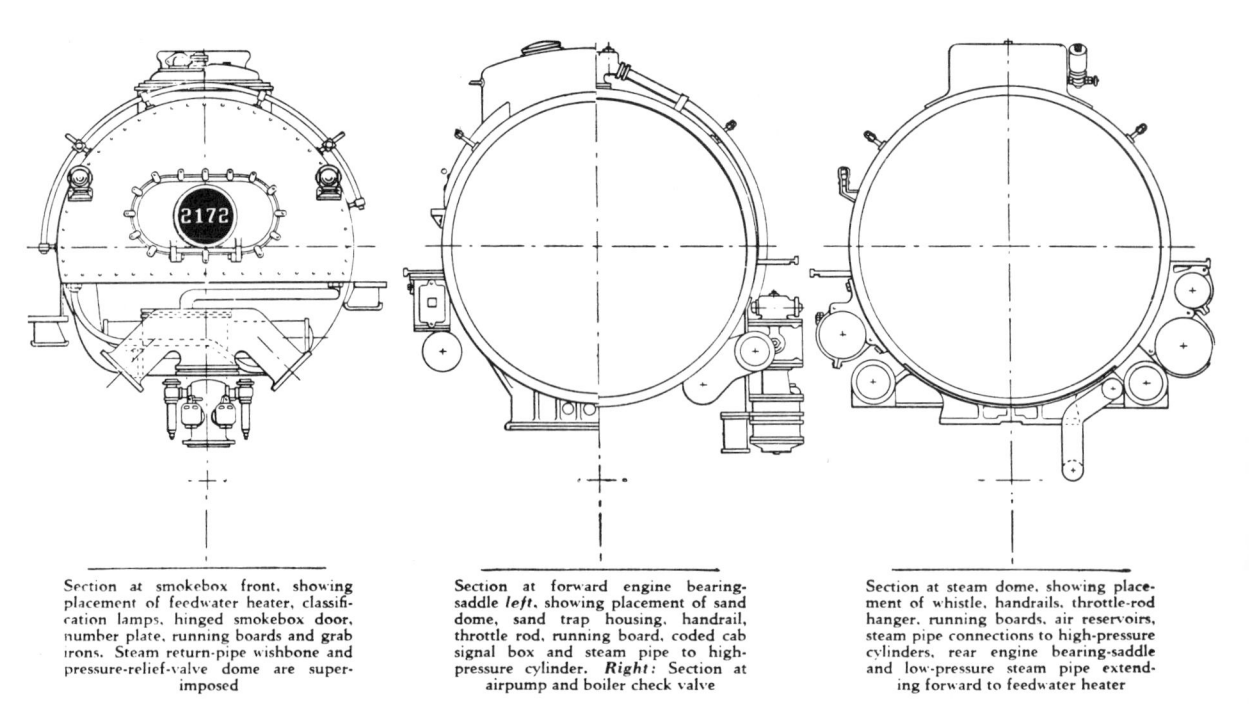

**Section at forward engine bearing-saddle** *left*, showing placement of sand dome, sand trap housing, handrail, throttle rod, running board, coded cab signal box and steam pipe to high-pressure cylinder. *Right*: Section at airpump and boiler check valve

**Section at steam dome,** showing placement of whistle, handrails, throttle-rod hanger, running boards, air reservoirs, steam pipe connections to high-pressure cylinders, rear engine bearing-saddle and low-pressure steam pipe extending forward to feedwater heater

57

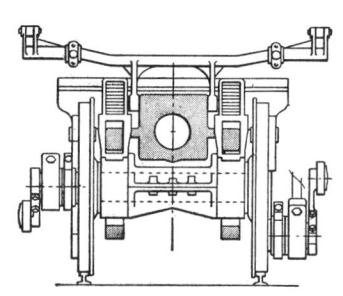

Number 3, or main drivers, looking forward to bearing saddle support

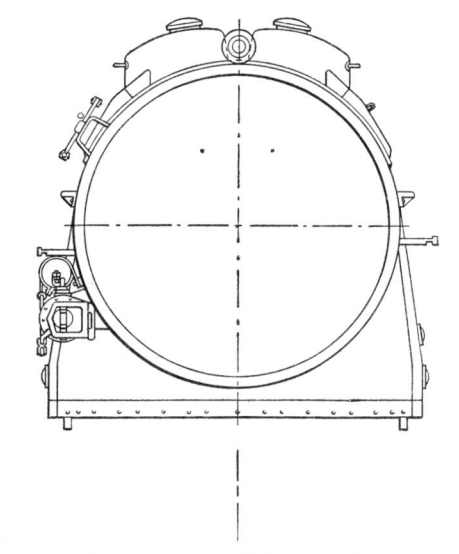

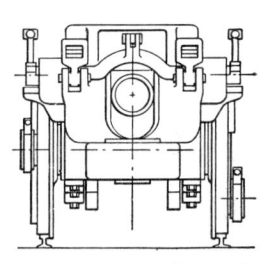

Rear elevation, looking forward from connecting pin tongue

*Below:* Rear view of rear engine

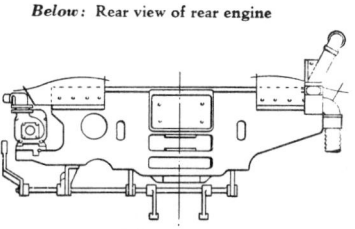

Section at rear sand domes, showing placement of collector pipe, throttle compensating lever, handrails, running boards and power-reverse gear. Twin sand domes conform to outer contour of forward, single-dome housing. Firebox cross-section is at forward end

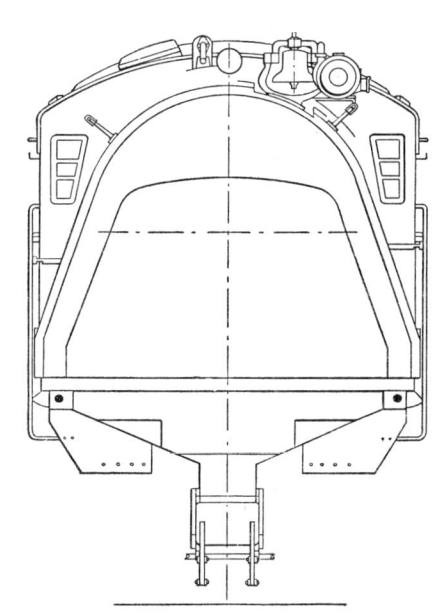

Section at cab front with low-water alarm, headlight generator and recessed bell superimposed. Firebox and ashpan contours are at rear hopper; note recess for driving wheels. Relatively small cab adds much to impression of size created by Y-6 Class; actually the boiler is not much larger than those applied to large 4-8-4s, including N&W's own J Class

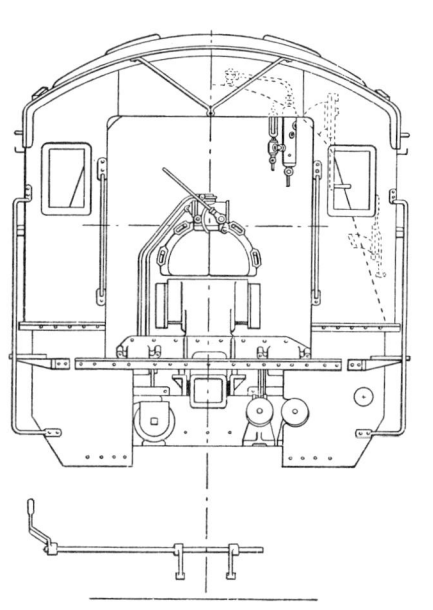

Section at rear of cab, showing placement of firedoors, throttle lever, water column and reverse lever. Under cab detail, including grate-shaker cylinders, cold-water pipe and pump, are secured to rear engine bed.

58

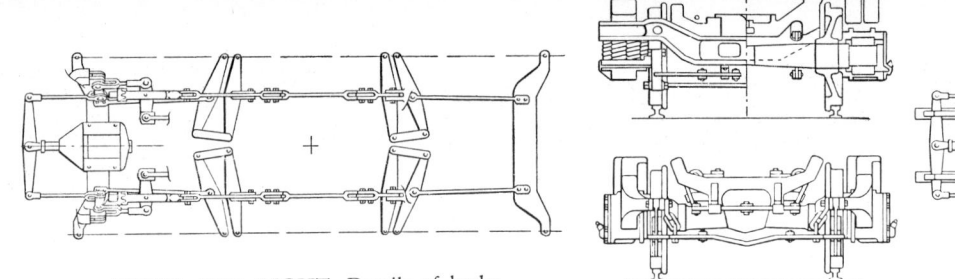

**ABOVE AND RIGHT:** Details of brake rigging and truck framing.

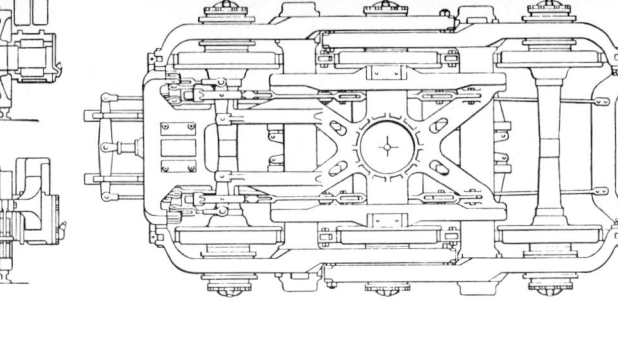

Rear elevation. Tender is 10 ft. 6 in. wide

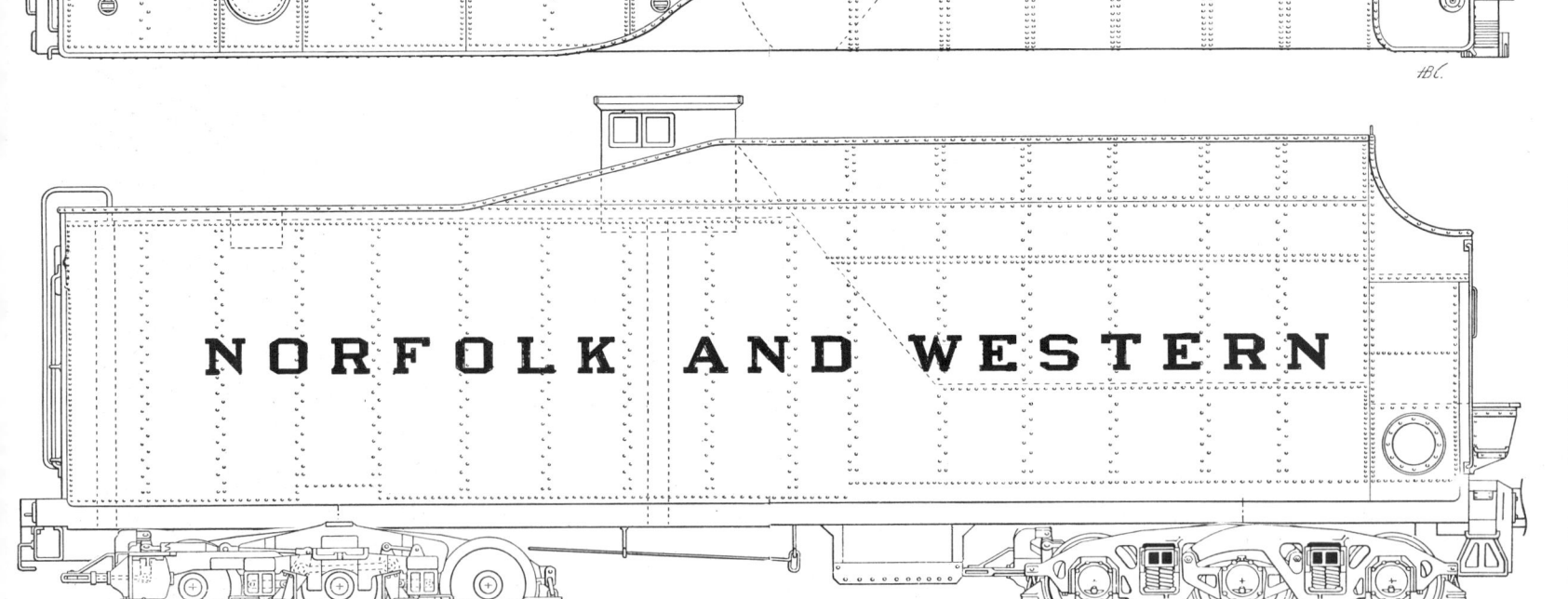

# Y6b Tender
30 tons coal, 22,000 gals. water

NOTE: The cutaway view of truck at rear of tender is actually the front truck. (Rear truck would be mirror image).

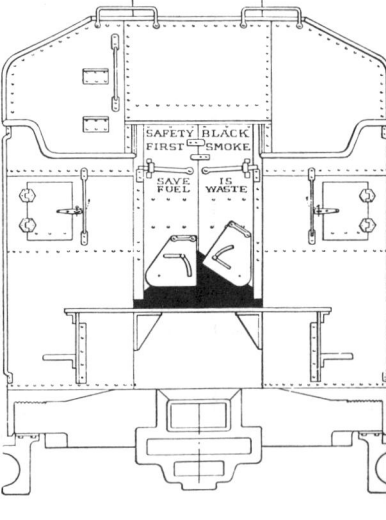

Scale: 3/16" = 1'0"

59

Workmen fit Y6b 2185 together in Roanoke Shops.  *N&W photo.*

LEFT: Helper 2161 blasts upgrade at — you guessed it — Blue Ridge, Virginia. *Frank G. Zahn photo.*

RIGHT: 2133 with canteen car assists a streamlined K2 departing from one of the N&W's numerous concrete coaling stages. *Collection of Allan Sherry.*

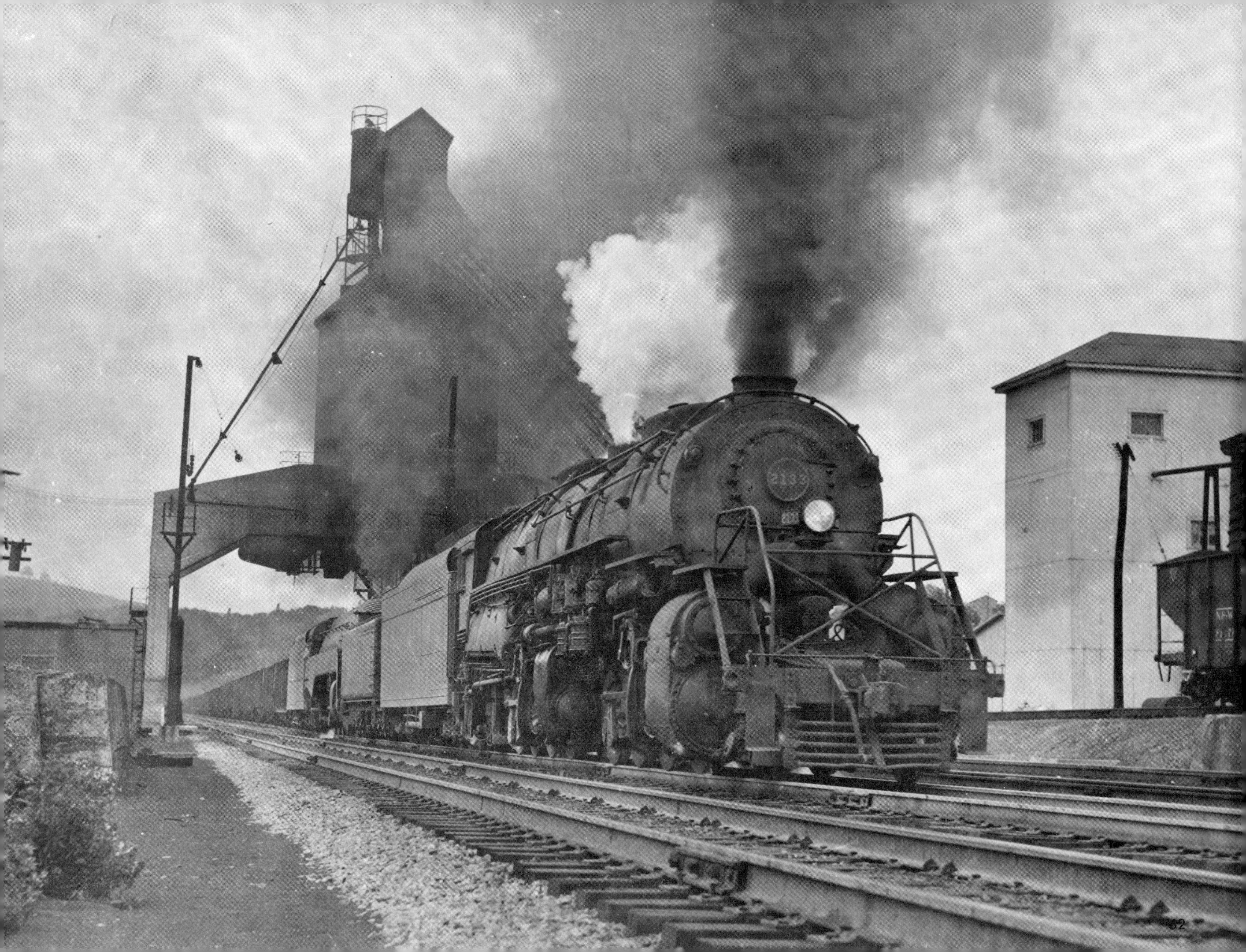
2133

In February, 1958, Don Ball, Jr. found Y6 2137 lugging 155 loads of coal into a lingering West Virginia sunset near Williamson.

Sister 2143 was caught with her front engine slipping badly while switching at a mine. *Don Ball, Jr.*

65

LEFT: Crewmen find welcome relief when Y6 2125 shoots into the fresh air and exits Montgomery Tunnel, Virginia on a July day in 1955. *Collection of Harold K. Vollrath.*

RIGHT: Road diesels came to the Norfolk and Western so suddenly that photos of the two types of motive power in cooperation are comparatively rare, and we are indebted to Don Ball, Jr. for this view of a Y6, three Alco DL-701's and caboose. Fittingly, the diesels which replaced the Y6's wore utilitarian hoods, not slick sports suits.

A hostler tops off 2130's sand supply under the Roanoke Coaling Tower.
*N&W photo.*

67

# 4-8-4 J

The J-class 4-8-4's were the result of the N&W's search for a fitting successor to the well-regarded K2 4-8-2's performing the road's most taxing passenger assignments. That was quite a task, since the K2's in the event proved so useful that all were retained until the dieselization of the N&W two decades later! What the railway really needed was not so much more locomotive, but greater availability.

To meet this demand, the J's were designed with roller bearings on all loco and tender axles, as well as on the wrist and crank pins and valve gear. Mechanical lubricators were specified to reach 220 points and operate 1,300 miles without replenishment. On extended runs, only the roller bearings on the crank and wrist pins needed attention at 500 mile intervals. The new locos went an average of 238,000 miles before classified repairs became necessary, and drew assignments approximating 15,000 miles per month — quite respectable considering wartime traffic density, the rugged profile of the N&W main, and the limited length of through loco runs.

ABOVE: 604 eases out of Roanoke in October, 1950 in charge of the daytime coach streamliner *Powhatan Arrow* linking Norfolk and Cincinnati. Pursuant to regional custom, colored passengers rode up front — those with through tickets were accommodated in the first car, while local travellers "shared" the second car, a partitioned coach, with whites. *Collection of Charles E. Winters.*

Road Numbers and Years Built by Roanoke Shops:
J class
600-603 (1941)
604 (1942, with trailer truck booster)
J1 class
605-610 (1943, not streamlined)
(J1 class streamlined and reclassed as J's, 1945)
J class
611-613 (1950)
(Boiler pressure of locos 600-610 later increased to 300 psi).

| Driv. Diam. | Total Loco Weight | Weight On Drivers | Cylinders Bore x Stroke | Boiler Pressure | Tractive Effort |
|---|---|---|---|---|---|
| 70" | 494,000 lbs. | 288,000 lbs. | 27"x32" | 275 psi | 73,300 lbs. |
| 70" | 494,000 lbs. | 288,000 lbs. | 27"x32" | 275 psi | 85,500 lbs.* |
| 70" | 494,000 lbs. | 288,000 lbs. | 27"x32" | 275 psi | 73,300 lbs. |
| 70" | 494,000 lbs. | 288,000 lbs. | 27"x32" | 300 psi | 80,000 lbs. |

*With booster engaged.

ABOVE: 602 leans into a curve with the westbound *Powhatan Arrow* on a muggy May morning in 1958. Note the condensation on the cool flanks of the tender. *Frank Zahn photo.*

RIGHT: The original member of class J was sadly relegated to freight service when Don Ball, Jr. took this portrait. A "doghouse" shelter has been tacked on the tender deck to house the brakeman.

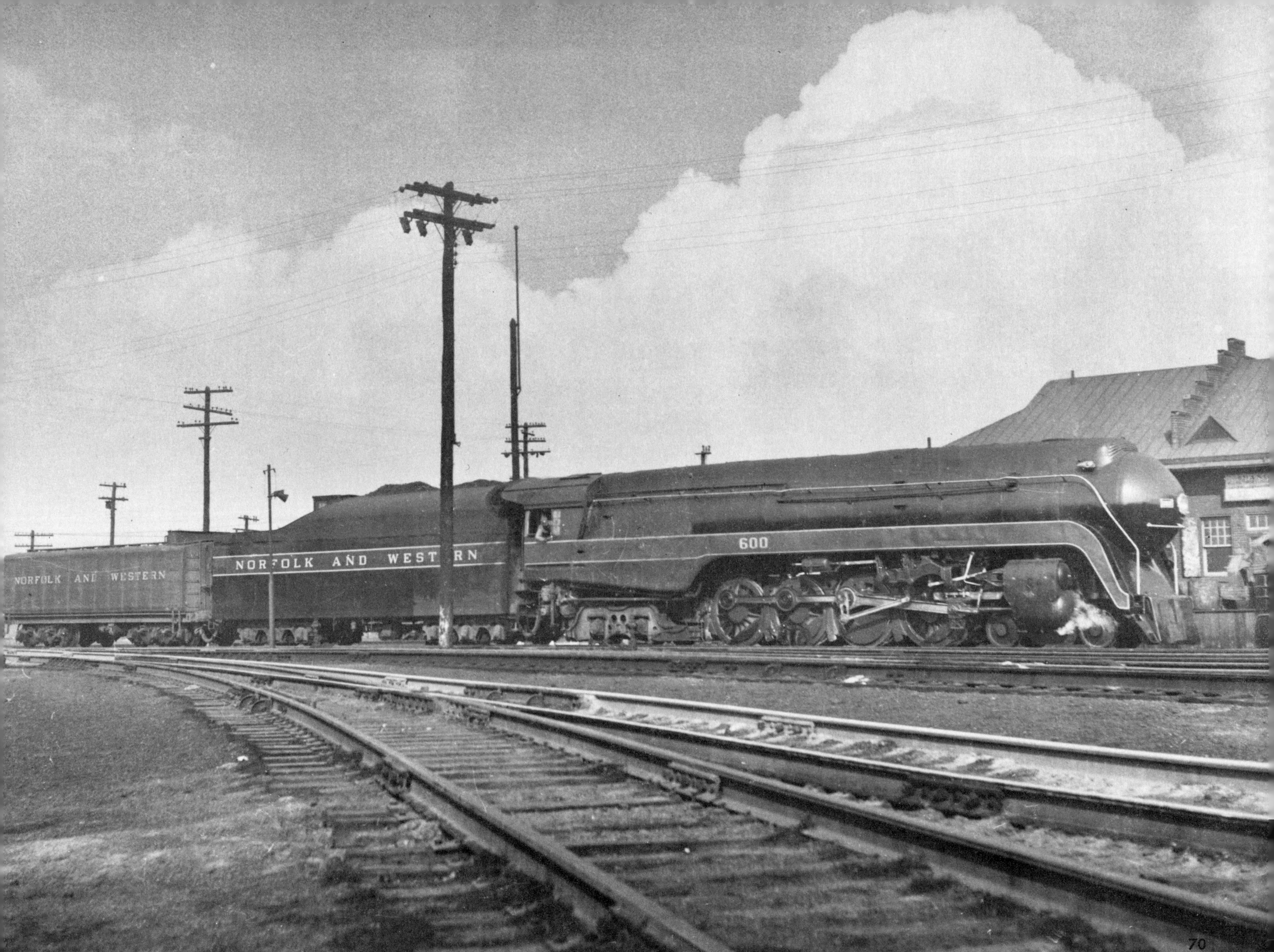
NORFOLK AND WESTERN
NORFOLK AND WESTERN
600

# The J in Perspective

This fine plan is basically a model builder's general arrangement drawing once distributed by the Norfolk and Western. However, the proportions of the cab window and firebox have been corrected to conform to the actual appearance of the J's as built.

COLOR SCHEDULE:
Lettering and striping dulux gold.
Twenty-inch band tuscan red.
Balance of locomotive black.

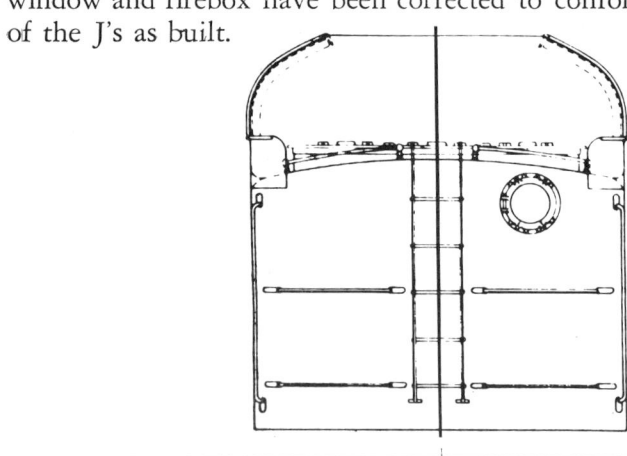

REAR VIEW TENDER

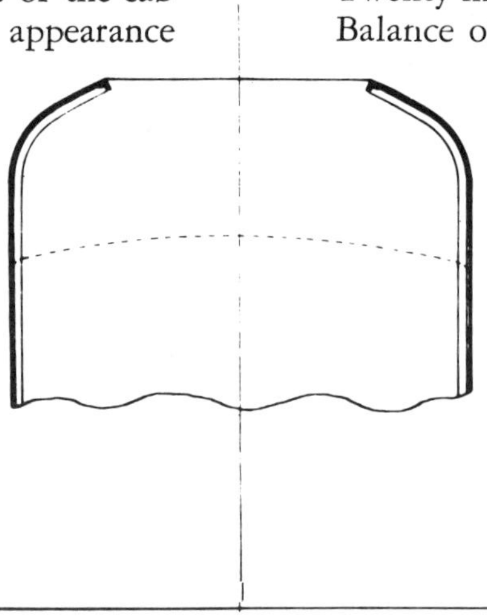

CROSS SECTION TENDER

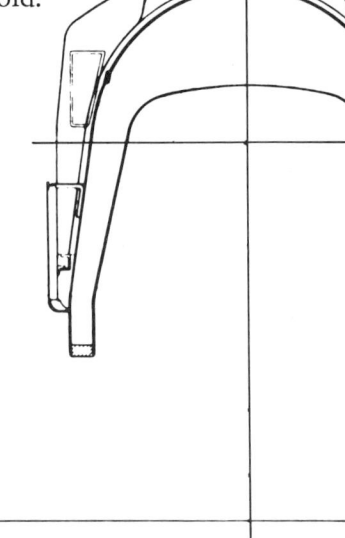

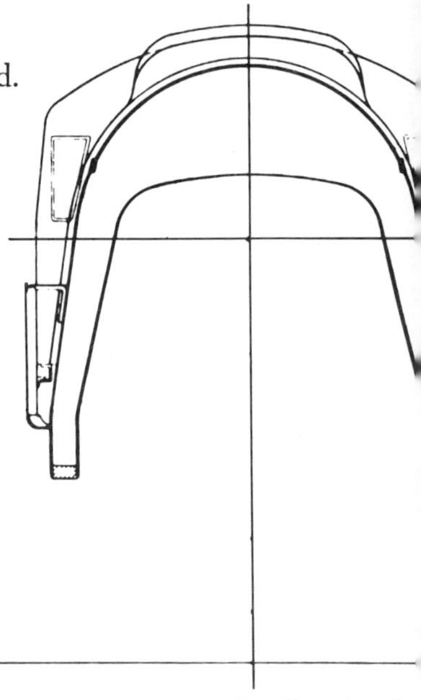

CROS

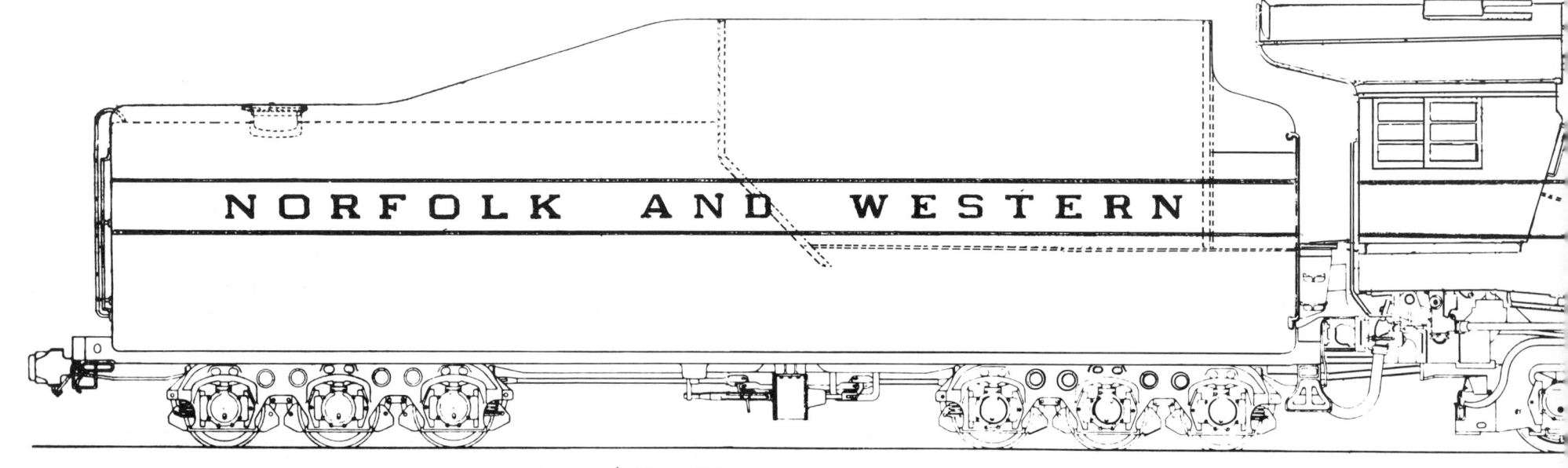

NORFOLK AND WESTERN

Scale: 3/16" = 1'0"
Full size for S gauge

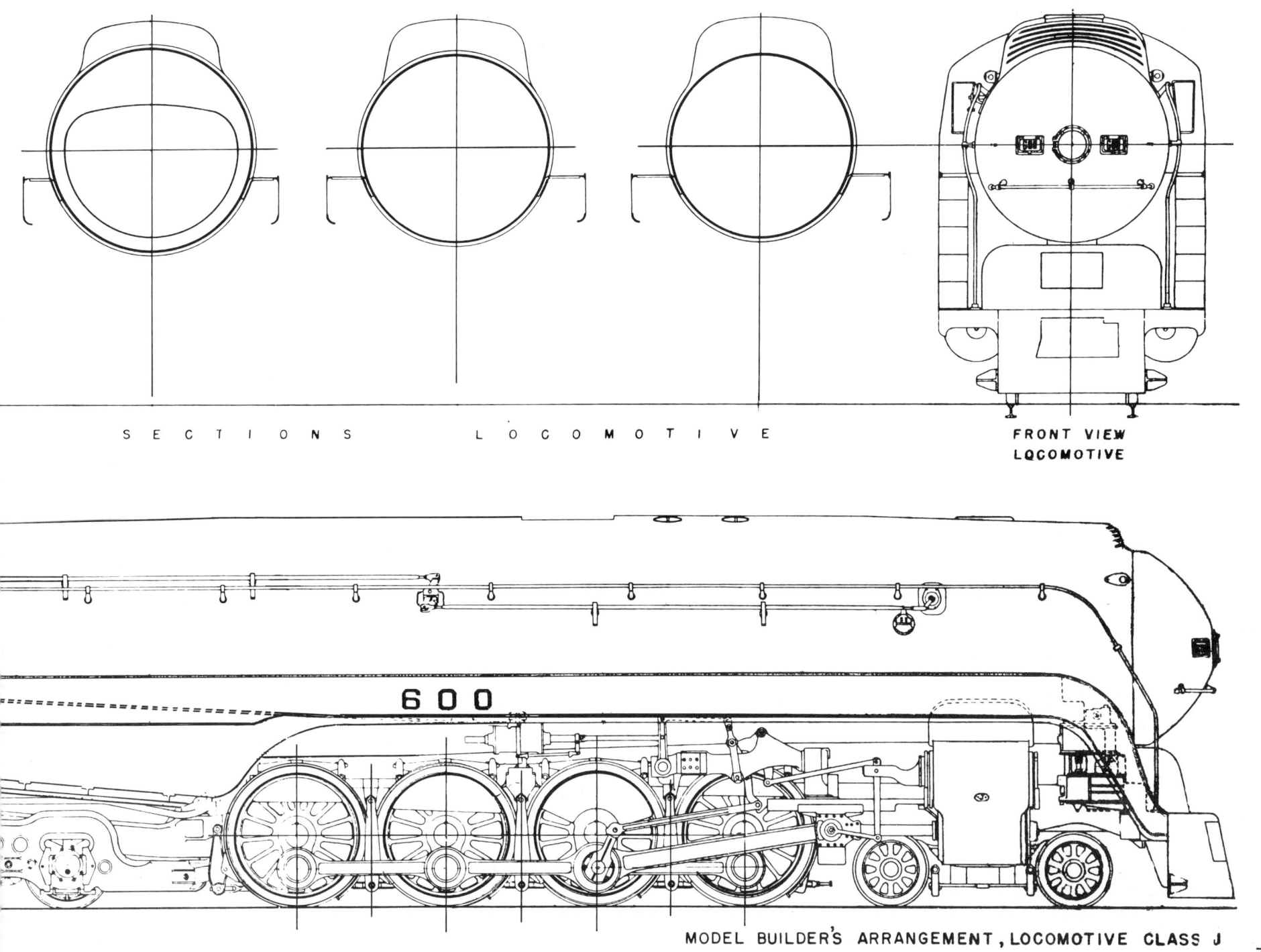

SECTIONS LOCOMOTIVE

FRONT VIEW LOCOMOTIVE

600

MODEL BUILDER'S ARRANGEMENT, LOCOMOTIVE CLASS J

# 4-8-4 J1

Few fans realize that six Norfolk and Western 4-8-4's were not always streamlined. Locos 605-610, 1943 Roanoke grads, lacked the nose cone, skyline casing and skirts. After V-J day, they received all the frills and were re-classed as ordinary J locos. RIGHT: This photo from the collection of Harold Vollrath shows 605 fresh from the shop. We regret we were unable to obtain a view of the right side of a J1, but we are quite proud to reproduce the rare diagram below.

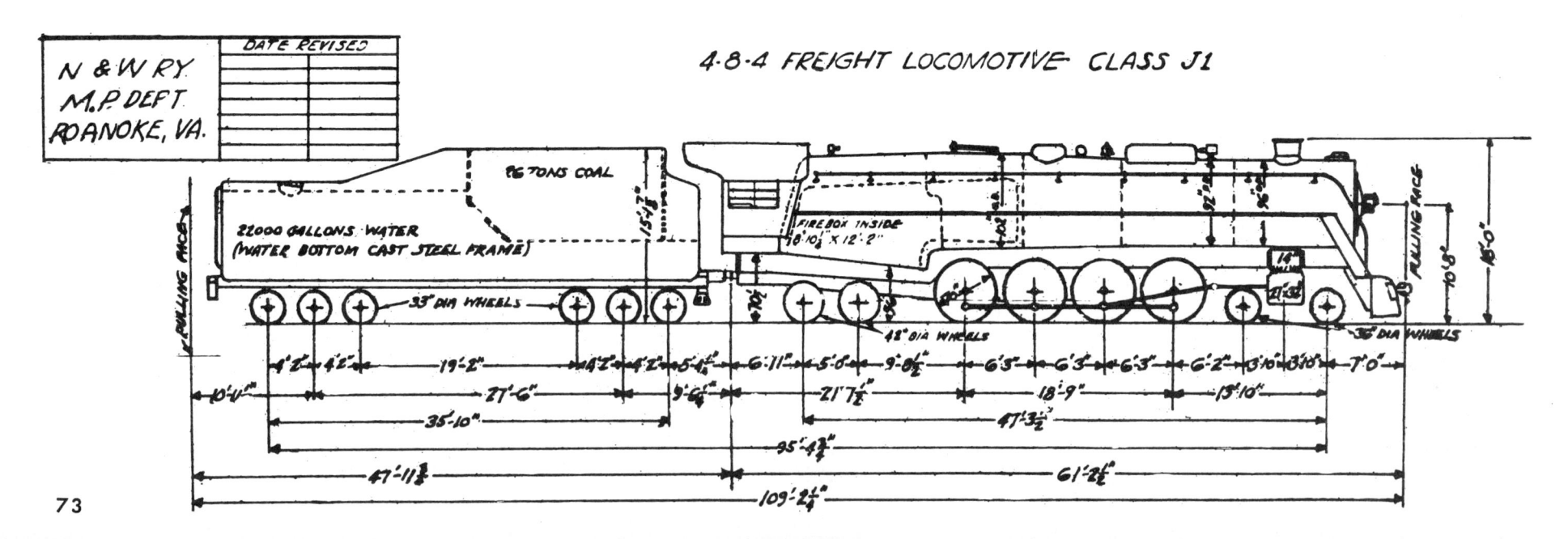

Frank Zahn found 609, a J1 in mufti, hustling an abbreviated *Powhatan Arrow* westbound through Crewe, Virginia on a brisk December morning in 1958.

The three postwar J's were outshopped with a working boiler pressure of 300 psi, and the resultant tractive effort of 80,000 pounds made them the mightiest of 4-8-4's anywhere. At Bristol, Virginia, in 1956 loco 611, the subject of our cover painting has just put some of that power to use to retrieve a Southern F-3 which fell down on the job. *Collection of Harold K. Vollrath.*

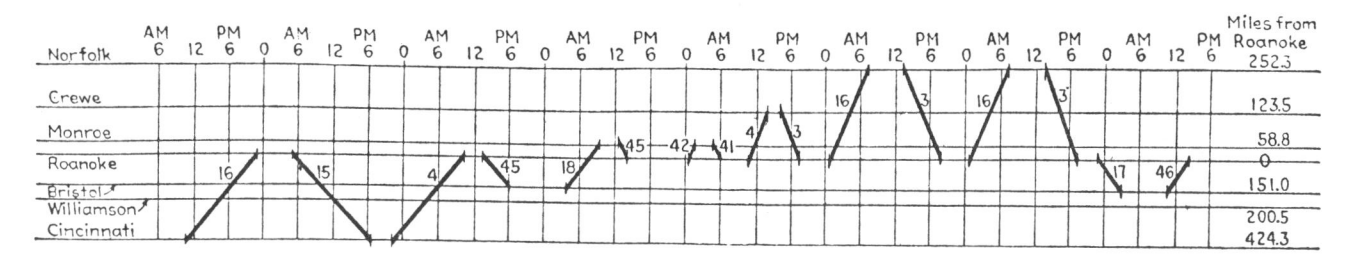

| District | Train No. | Mileage | No. Cars |
|---|---|---|---|
| Cincinnati-Roanoke | 16 | 424.3 | 11 |
| Roanoke-Cincinnati | 15 | 424.3 | 8 |
| Cincinnati-Roanoke | 4 | 424.3 | 14 |
| Roanoke-Bristol | 45 | 151.0 | 15 |
| Bristol-Monroe | 18 | 209.8 | 14 |
| Monroe-Roanoke | 45 | 58.8 | 14 |
| Roanoke-Monroe | 42 | 58.8 | 10 |
| Monroe-Roanoke | 41 | 58.8 | 13 |
| Roanoke-Crewe | 4 | 123.5 | 14 |
| Crewe-Roanoke | 3 | 123.5 | 9 |
| Roanoke-Norfolk | 16 | 252.3 | 14 |
| Norfolk-Roanoke | 3 | 252.3 | 9 |
| Roanoke-Norfolk | 16 | 252.3 | 17 |
| Norfolk-Roanoke | 3 | 252.3 | 12 |
| Roanoke-Bristol | 17 | 151.0 | 14 |
| Bristol-Roanoke | 46 | 151.0 | 15 |
| Total locomotive mileage (seven days) | | 3,368.3 | |

**The Runs Made by One Class J Locomotive in Seven Days' Operation Are Plotted on the Above Chart—The Details Are Shown in the Table**

J 613, the final 4-8-4 built in North America steps smartly out of the Bluefield depot with a fifteen-car *Pocahontas* bound for Cincinnati. *Marvin H. Cohen photo.*

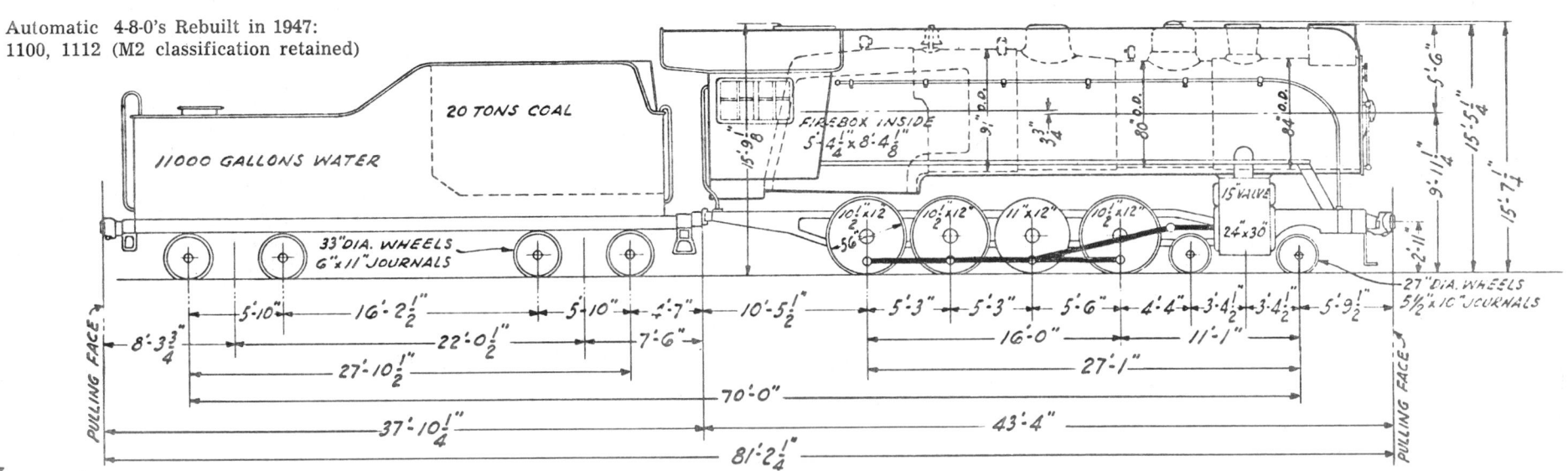

# 4-8-0
# M2 Automatic

In 1947, the N&W faced the reality that most of the locos in use as switchers were no longer economical to operate. Two M2 4-8-0's were modernized in an attempt to create a steam switcher with the high availability and low maintenance demands of diesels, but with lower initial cost. The 1100 and 1112 received automatic boiler pressure controls and safety and standby devices to minimize the need for human attendance. Hennesey lubricators were fitted to the drivers, and each received a tender holding two days' supply of coal and enough water for eight hours running. A longer combustion chamber, over-fire air jets, a low-speed stoker, and a turbine-driven draft fan were among the changes made to increase thermal efficiency. The locos worked as expected, but the availability of ex-C&O 0-8-0's in 1950 made further experimentation pointless. RIGHT: 1112 at the end in Roanoke, 1951. *Collection of Harold K. Vollrath.*

| Driv. Diam. | Total Loco Weight | Weight On Drivers | Cylinders Bore x Stroke | Boiler Pressure | Tractive Effort |
|---|---|---|---|---|---|
| 56" | 279,530 lbs. | 239,530 lbs. | 24"x30" | 200 psi | 52,457 lbs. |

Automatic 4-8-0's Rebuilt in 1947:
1100, 1112 (M2 classification retained)

ABOVE: Pristine Automatic M2 1100 at Roanoke in 1947.

# 0-8-0
# S1

In 1950, the Chesapeake & Ohio management made the precipitant decision to dieselize yard service, and their C-16 0-8-0's of U.S.R.A. design were out of work when less than two years old. The Norfolk and Western snapped up 30 for $45,000 each, and also acquired the blueprints. Roanoke built a total of 45 copies of the C&O locos over the next few years, inexpensively meeting the requirement for a new fleet of switching locomotives.

S1 class
255-284 (Baldwin, 1948 for C&O, same numbers)
S1a class
200-214 (Roanoke Shops, 1951)
215-229 (Roanoke Shops, 1952)
230-244 (Roanoke Shops, 1953)

Marv Cohen found the 265 switching at the Roanoke depot in 1954.

| Driv. Diam. | Total Loco Weight | Weight On Drivers | Cylinders Bore x Stroke | Boiler Pressure | Tractive Effort |
|---|---|---|---|---|---|
| 52" | 247,000 lbs. | 247,000 lbs. | 25"x28" | 220 psi | 62,932 lbs. |

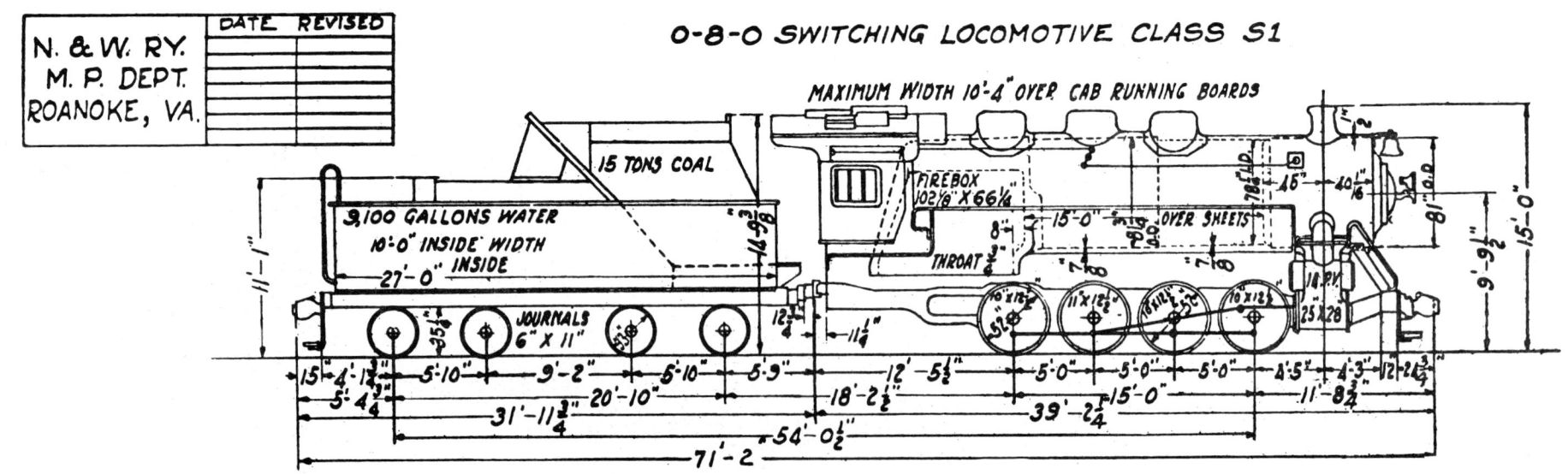

This dingy Chesapeake & Ohio C-16 was less than a year old when photographed at Richmond. Finding an N&W 0-8-0 in this unkempt condition was almost impossible!

Here's one of the bargains at Roanoke in 1952. The most important alteration so far is the addition of overfire air jets to the sides of the firebox. *Both photos, collection of H. K. Vollrath.*

This C&O veteran manifests all the improvements made by the N&W. From front to rear, we find a larger headlight, cinder screen on the stack, over-fire air jets, extended coal bunker, and clerestory tender deck indicating increased water capacity. *Bill Jernstrom photo.*

# S1a

The N&W-built 0-8-0's were best distinguished from their C&O cousins by their all-welded tenders. These tanks packed an additional 3,900 gallons of water, with only a six-foot increase in length. RIGHT: Copy 231 was colorfully decked out with a graphite-and-oil finished boiler and cylinder saddle when photographed at Columbus in 1955. *Collection of Harold K. Vollrath.*

The last six serviceable S1a's, 208, 215, 217, 231, 234, and 235 were eventually renumbered 290-295 to free up another block of numbers for road switchers on order. Shortly after midnight on May 7, 1960 S1a 291 completed a switching trick at Williamson and a hostler dropped her fire. No N&W steamer was thereafter recalled to service.

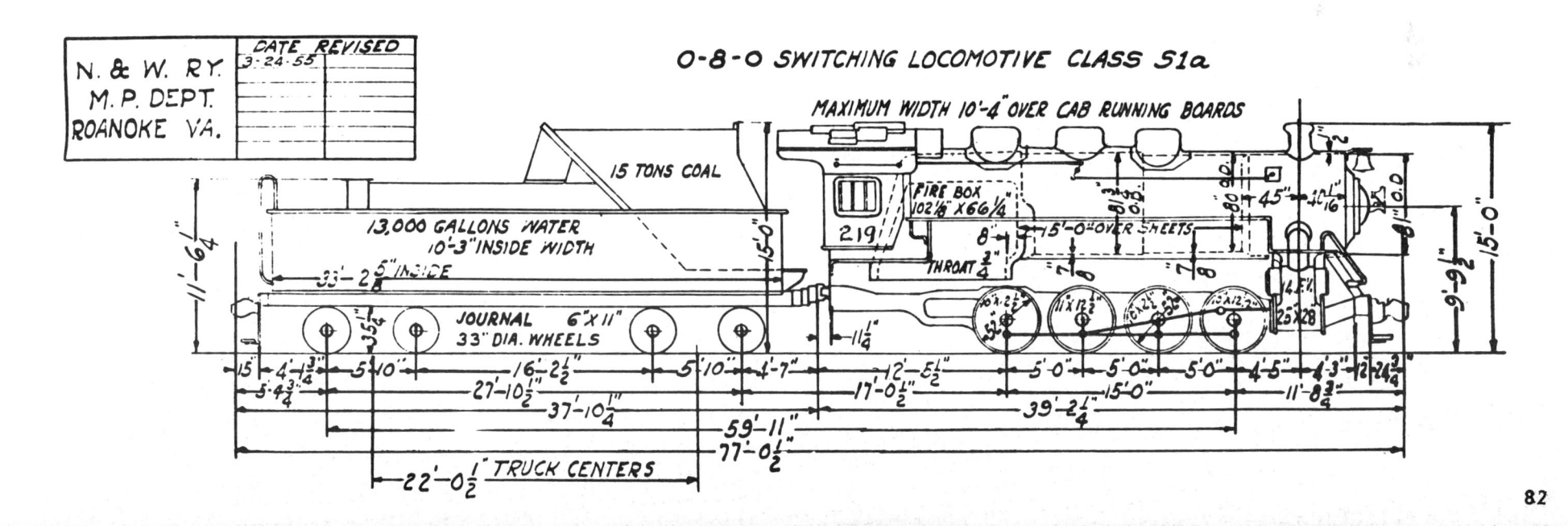

**THE LAST OF MANY:** S1a 244 proved to be the last Roanoke-built locomotive, and the final steamer constructed for service in America. Few were surprised that such laurels went to the N&W. *Company photo, December, 1953*

233 assembles a train in another of Don Ball's remarkable photos of N&W steam power at work.

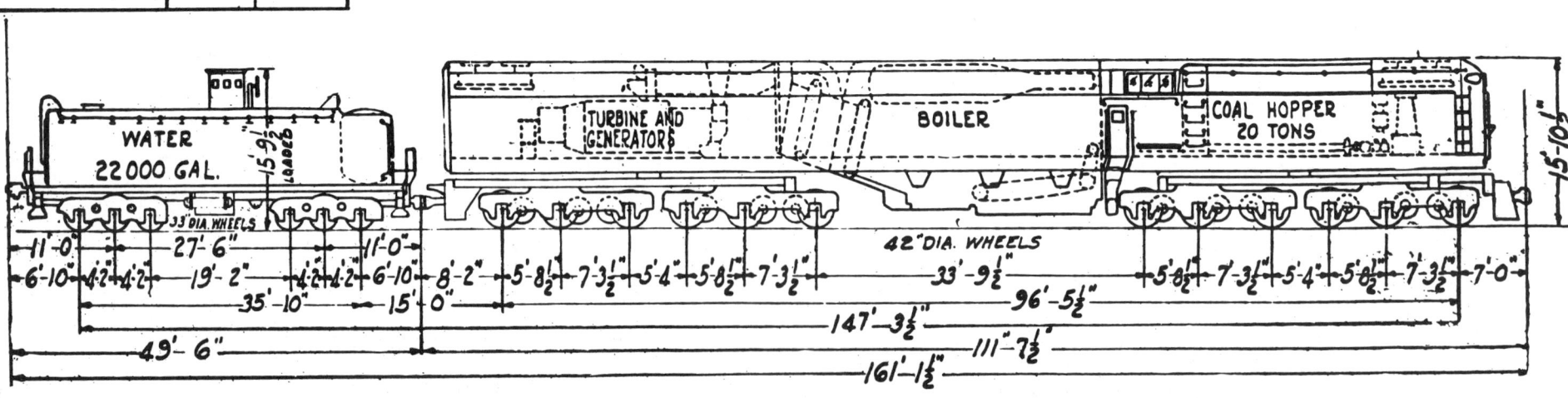

# C-C+C-C TE1

In 1954, the N&W, Westinghouse Electric, the Baldwin-Lima-Hamilton Corporation and boiler-builders Babcock & Wilcox made one final attempt to develop a more efficient coal-fueled steam locomotive. The monstrous steam turbine experimental was officially identified as 2300, but was known to railroaders and onlookers as the "Jawn Henry", or simply "Big Jawn".

The diagram below shows the facilities arrangement, right down to the massive traction motors on each of twelve axles. That continuous tractive effort rating of 144,000 pounds was, by the way, a conservative indication of the loco's capacity.

The mighty loco's durable traction motors could sustain enormous overloads for short time periods. What the loco's true capacity was, we don't know, but on one memorable occasion while in helper service, Jawn telescoped a steel-underframe caboose over a tank car as a small indication of his prowess.

Up to about 12 m.p.h., Big Jawn bested the Y6b and A locos in both tractive effort and horsepower! Better yet, the new behemoth hauled more freight for less fuel cost than the competing Y6b's over the hilly Radford and Pocahontas divisions between Roanoke, Bluefield, and Williamson. Savings relative to the operation of an A over the Scioto division between Williamson and Portsmouth were equally impressive, though the A's brought the freight over the road about 15% faster than the TE1 whose turbine reached maximum allowable r.p.m.'s at a road speed of 41.5 m.p.h.

| 2300 Built 1954 by Baldwin-Lima-Hamilton | Total Loco Wt. (On Drivers) 818,000 lbs. | Tender Wt. (Loaded) 364,100 lbs. | Weight Of Engine & Tender 1,182,100 lbs. | Continuous T.E. (at 9 m.p.h.) 144,000 lbs. | Boiler Pressure 600 psi | Traction Motors 12 | Driv. Diam. 42" |

OPPOSITE: Big Jawn with auxiliary tender and dynamometer car during testing in October, 1954. *Collection of Harold K. Vollrath.*

BELOW: Brute strength compared — the respective merits of the TE1, A and Y6b.

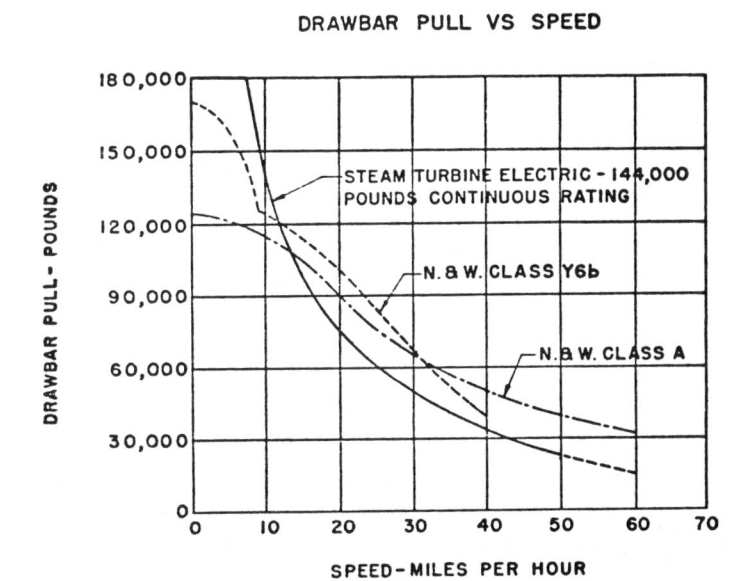

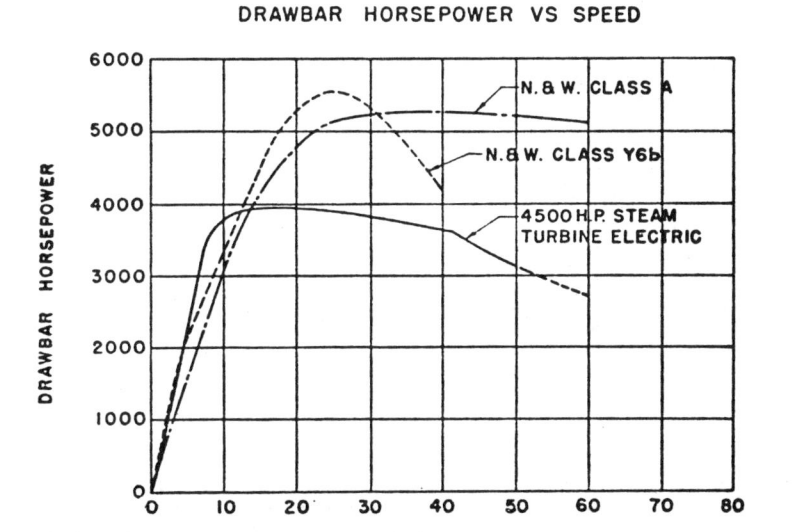

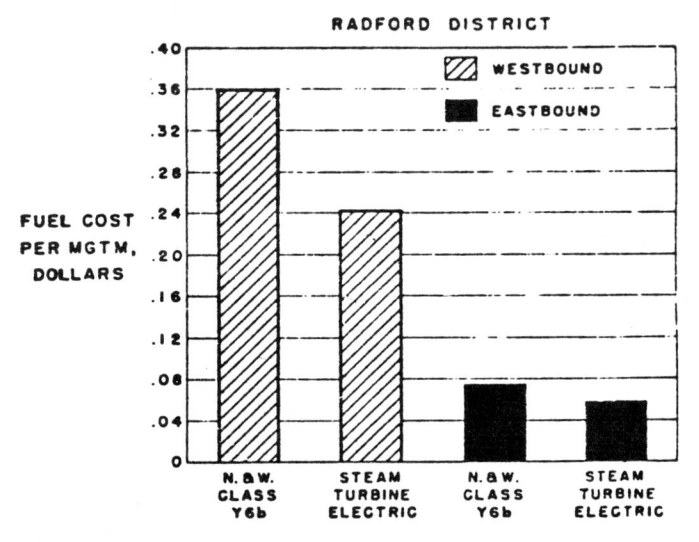

GIANTS' APPETITES:

Above, Roanoke to Bluefield. Beneath, Williamson to Portsmouth.

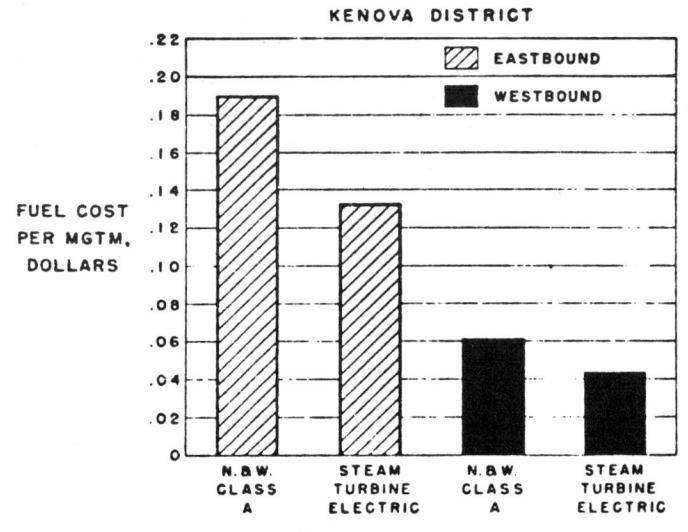

OPPOSITE: Jawn in his glory.

POSTSCRIPT: Giants, like most mutants, have a limited life expectancy. Jawn made his point, but his high production costs precluded duplication, and he went to retirement on New Year's Day, 1958.

# Part 3: Wandering Giants

One of the practical results of the N&W's motive power policies was that many unpopular or inefficient locomotives were available for resale to less discriminating owners. The rotund K3 4-8-2's are a case in point. Here are their N&W numbers and subsequent service identities:

| N&W | D&RGW | RF&P | W&LE | NKP |
|-----|-------|------|------|-----|
| 200 | ——— | 515 | 6801 | 841 |
| 201 | ——— | 516 | 6802 | 842 |
| 202 | ——— | 517 | 6803 | 843 |
| 203 | ——— | 518 | 6804 | 844 |
| 204 | ——— | 519 | 6805 | 845 |
| 205 | ——— | 520 | 6806 | 846 |
| 206 | 1550 | ——— | 6807 | 847 |
| 207 | 1551 | ——— | 6808 | 848 |
| 208 | 1552 | ——— | 6809 | 849 |
| 209 | 1553 | ——— | 6810 | 850 |

*All three photos this page, collection of Harold K. Vollrath.*

The Rio Grande became a refuge for two classes of elderly N&W articulateds during World War Two. N&W Z1a's 1453 and 1457 became locos 3350 and 3351 in the D&RGW class L-76. Y2's 1701, 1722, 1724, 1728, 1729, 1730, 1710, 1727, 1706, 1709, 1713, 1714, 1719, 1725, and 1726 also wandered West to become D&RGW's L-109's 3550-3564, respectively.

Some Z1b's were sold, but stayed much closer to home. 1396 retained its number when sold to the Tennessee Central, but Interstate had no such tolerance for astronomical numbers, and renumbered N&W 1426 to 24. *All photos on these two pages are from the collection of Harold K. Vollrath.*

Eight Y3's were sold to the Santa Fe in 1943, and the seven survivors of this group returned to the Blue Ridge in 1948 after purchase by the Virginian Railway. The N&W/ATSF/VGN identities of these seven were: 2021/179/0738, 2022/1791/739, 2026/1792/737, 2015/1793/740, 2014/1794736, 2029/1795/741 and finally 2035/1796/742. N&W 2042 was scraped as ATSF 1797.

Pennsy HH-1's 373-378 were formerly N&W locos 2000, 2008, 2027, 2034, 2036, and 2047. ABOVE: 374 takes a drink at Columbus, O.
The other wartime Y3 sale resulted in the metamorphosis of N&W numbers 2030, 2020, 2025, 2041, and 2013 into locos 3670-3674 of the Union Pacific.

90

# Part 4: Smaller Surplus

Loco 108 of N&W subsidiary Chesapeake Western was number 812, a W2 2-8-0.

Another W2, the 869, retained its N&W number on the High Point, Thomasville, and Denton Railroad.

Many lighter N&W locomotives were sold to short lines and regional carriers throughout the Southeast in the 'thirties and 'forties. We wish space and time allowed us to document each such transfer, but subsequent movements of these locos after they left the Norfolk and Western are very difficult to trace, which is really not surprising to us railfans who know of the informality of these little lines down South. Nonetheless, we thought many N&W enthusiasts would enjoy this representative sampling.

N&W W2 716 was little affected by its transfer to the Winston-Salem Southbound, a property jointly owned by the N&W and Atlantic Coast Line.

Through two sales and a merger, N&W M 485 became a High Point, Thomasville and Denton loco of the same number, then Atlanta, Birmingham, and Coast number 34, before finally winding up as Atlantic Coast Line 7034.

*Again, all these photos are from the collection of Harold K. Vollrath.*

Winston-Salem Southbound 200 began life as one of those many M1's for which the Norfolk & Western had so little regard.

Not surprisingly, Durham and Southern 1140 bore the same number as a Norfolk and Western M2.

92

# Part 5: Models Made

MANY MODELS of Norfolk and Western prototype steam locos have been offered, or will be marketed in the near future.

The least expensive and most popular have been the plastic and metal Y6b's built in 1:160 proportion (N gauge) by Rowa of West Germany and in 1:87.1 proportion (HO gauge) by Rivarossi of Italy. These locos have been imported and distributed in the United States by Model Rectifier Corporation and Associated Hobby Manufacturers, respectively.

Fine Japanese-made brass models of three N&W locos have been imported in years past in 1:48 proportion (O scale). Pacific Fast Mail brought in a U.S.R.A. Heavy Mountain like the N&W K2 class, and the late Max Gray offered a J and a Y6b.

HO enthusiasts have had a choice of many N&W-prototype brass models. Pacific Fast Mail has imported the C&O C-16 0-8-0, an A, a J, and a Y6b, as well as an auxiliary tender. Akane once sold the U.S.R.A. Heavy 4-8-2 and the 2-8-8-2. LMB brought in the M-class 4-8-0. Gem offered a J, painted and lettered, or in plain brass. Northwest Short Line has recently imported no less than three variations of the E2 4-6-2, plus the popular water canteen. NWSL shortly expects to release a model of the massive TE1 "Jawn Henry", to be followed by models of the classes W2, W6, V1, M and M1.

We regret to inform you that the finely-detailed representation of an S1a shown on this page has never been offered for sale. This marvelous model was built to ½" scale in England for display in the Smithsonian Institution.